Incredible *Life*

**Top Experts Reveal
How to Create Yours**

PowerDynamics
PUBLISHING

PowerDynamics Publishing
San Francisco, California
www.powerdynamicspub.com

ISBN: 978-0-9644906-8-0

Library of Congress Control Number: 2010905689

Printed in the United States of America on acid-free paper.

We dedicate this book

to you, our readers, who want
to lead an *Incredible Life.*
We know that you are ready to
take steps to create positive changes
in your life—and we celebrate
your commitment to being the best,
most incredible person you can be!

The Co-Authors of Incredible Life

Table of Contents

Acknowledgements

Gratitude is a key part of creating an incredible life. Before we share our wisdom and experience with you, we have a few people to thank for turning our vision for this book into a reality.

This book is the brilliant concept of Caterina Rando, the founder of PowerDynamics Publishing and a respected business strategist and coach, with whom many of us have worked to grow our businesses. Working closely with many life coaches, consultants and other professionals, she realized how valuable the knowledge they possessed would be to those people wanting to create an incredible life for themselves. The result was putting our ideas into a comprehensive book on achieving an incredible life.

Without Caterina's "take action" spirit, her positive attitude and her commitment to excellence, you would not be reading this book of which we are all so proud. She was supported by a truly dedicated team who worked diligently to put together the best possible book for you. We are truly grateful for everyone's stellar contribution.

To Valerie Camarda, marketing communications maven who served as the copy editor and project manager for this book, we appreciate your patient guidance, thoughtful advice and genuine enthusiasm for our work, and we are truly grateful.

To Ruth Schwartz, with her many years of experience and wisdom, who served as an ongoing guide throughout the project, your leadership of our production team was invaluable.

To Tammy Tribble, our brilliant illustrator and one of our fellow contributing authors, we thank you for creating the clean, crisp look for our book cover and interior illustrations.

To Tricia Principe, our graphic designer extraordinaire who designed the interior pages you are now reading, we thank you.

To LynAnn King and Laura Piester, who were instrumental in identifying each of us as an expert in our respective fields, we thank you for being such great matchmakers.

To Bernie Burson, who provided us with a keen eye and an elegant touch, thank you for your support and contribution and for making us read so perfectly on paper.

To Karen Gargiulo who provided us with her sharp attention on our punctuation, grammar and consistency, thank you for your support and contribution.

The Co-Authors of Incredible Life

Introduction

Congratulations! You have opened a resource that is jam-packed with great ideas that will improve your life in ways you cannot yet imagine. You are about to discover the secrets to achieving an *incredible life.*

Your personal successes in life come as a result of wanting the best life possible. As top experts in each of our respective specialties, we've joined together to give you insightful guidance and advice learned through years of study and consulting with our clients and working with our colleagues.

You have probably seen how even small changes in perspective and behavior can transform and uplift your life. In the following pages you will learn:

- How understanding what your body and mind need to thrive can help get you through the most challenging of days

- How believing in your abilities will give you the self-confidence to reach far beyond what you originally thought you could

- How to create a vision for your life and set the goals that will help bring your dreams to reality

- How you can have the life you want with direction, commitment and follow-through

All of the professionals you will meet in this book want you to achieve your *incredible life*. We have outlined for you our top tips and included the most expert advice we have to help you achieve your goals.

To get the most out of this book, read through it once cover to cover. Then go back and follow the tips that apply to you in the chapters most relevant to your current situation. Every improvement you make will get you closer to the life you really want and deserve.

Know that just learning what to do will not transform your life. You must take action and apply the strategies, tips and tactics we share in these pages. Apply the many tools we have provided in this book and you will reap many rewards. With our knowledge and your action, we are confident that, like our thousands of satisfied clients, you too will achieve an *incredible life*.

To your unlimited success!

The Co-Authors of Incredible Life

Discovering Your True Purpose
The Dance of the Ego and the Soul
By Erin Sarika Delaney, MA, CDC

"You are here to enable the divine purpose of the universe to unfold. That's how important you are."
—Eckhart Tolle, author of *The Power of Now*

I hear people say over and over again, "There is so much that needs to be done to transform and uplift this world, but I don't know where my place is within it. I don't know my purpose—how I can make a difference—what I am *really* meant to be doing?"

As a true purpose coach, I find that the majority of my clients are hungry for the truth of their soul to be revealed; to find the answers for their life from a deep place within them; to use their gifts, their knowledge, their passions, talents and skills in an optimal way. A way that not only brings them great meaning, but offers immense benefit to others as well, especially at a time when it seems most needed.

If you long to know your true purpose, then this chapter will assist you in delving within for the answers you seek and will offer you some tools to move you in the direction of discovering what you are uniquely designed to do. Knowing and living your true purpose brings greater clarity, peace of mind, and an inner connection and conviction to move toward that which is most true to your soul.

Ego and the Soul

Let us start by looking at two aspects of our psyche: the ego and the soul. Notice that I didn't say the ego *versus* the soul, which implies an opposition. In this chapter, we are going to play with the idea that the ego and the soul are not oppositional, but actually work hand in hand, weaving us through the inner and outer game of life, dancing in and out of each other to create our full human experience.

There are various definitions for the word ego. For the sake of what we are aiming for in this chapter, I define ego as the part of us that has a human form and a personality. It is composed of all of those things that create our identity—our physical appearance, our likes and dislikes, our life experiences, our thoughts and opinions, our education, our profession and so forth. Our ego has certain needs, like safety and stability, loving relationships, happiness, comfort, and a certain amount of respect and admiration.

The ego is not bad. It is necessary to help us function in this world. It's when we allow it to dominate and run our life that it causes problems and havoc. It's when the ego, consciously or unconsciously, blocks out the voice of the soul that complications and drama arise.

The soul is often defined as our essence; that which is continually guiding us in the direction of our higher purpose. In his book, *The Seat of the Soul*, published in 1989 by Simon & Schuster, Gary Zukav calls the soul "a positive, purposeful force at the core of your being." The soul seems to have a different function than the ego. Its function is for us to grow and develop and to fulfill the purpose of our birth.

Now that you have the distinction between the ego and the soul set for your journey, let's step into some highly practical and profound steps to assist you to tap into your soul. Generally, we do not need assistance to tap into our ego. We get plenty of support from the outside world around us. Where most people need some extra support is with the soul connection.

Going Within

I have found that a crucial first step in whatever I do is to take time, even a moment, to go within and connect with that sweet soul space. You may think that in order to go *within* you need to be in a tranquil, quiet place. Although that is ideal (and if you can find that space, by all means, please do so), I am more interested in helping you discover how to go within at any given moment in your life—even amidst a crowded, busy space; even in the thick of a traffic jam; even during a complicated meeting or a difficult interaction with another ego-soul. Here are three important steps you can access anywhere you are.

1. Become aware of your breath. Have you ever noticed that no matter how many healing-type books you read, workshops you attend or yoga classes you take, you are always reminded of the importance of the breath? Well, there's a good reason for that. When you become aware of your breath, your active mind automatically slows down and brings you to the present moment. Take a deep breath right now and release it slowly. Continue to take slow, natural, deep breaths in and out. You will likely notice a shift in your state from taking this one step.

2. Bring your attention inside. While you breathe, bring your attention to what Eckhart Tolle refers to as your *inner body*. Yes, that's right—in there with all the muscles, bones, organs and such. But move beyond these parts to the spaciousness within your body and let your mind settle in the area of your heart. This space is often referred to as the heart center or the heart chakra. By bringing your attention to your heart, you're gathering in the energy that you have been expending outward, now honing it inward to a focused point. You are allowing your mind to rest within.

3. Repeat a supportive word or phrase. You can now choose to take a further step, which is to repeat a supportive word or phrase, either out loud or silently. This is often known as a mantra or an affirmation. The Sanskrit word *mantra* can be defined as "sacred syllables that protect the mind." A mantra protects our mind from its limiting and contracting thought patterns. Traditionally, a mantra is in Sanskrit and given by a spiritual master. If you do not have such a mantra, then you can design one in your own language that resonates with what you most want to be, do or feel. For example, you may want to repeat a phrase like, *"I am at peace,"* with each in-breath and each out-breath. Or, *"I am perfect just as I am."* Or, *"I am forgiving."* Or, *"I am open to deeper wisdom."* You can also focus on repeating just one word, such as love, grace, tranquility, integrity, acceptance, brilliance, joy. What will you choose as your mantra?

From this still place, you can more easily feel or hear inner guidance. Accessing the still place within you is a profound way to begin any endeavor. Like anything important and valuable, it takes practice. Committing to this practice is likely to transform how you live and master your day-to-day life. Eventually, you can get to where you can step into all three at the same time—"Breath-Heart-Mantra."

Sometimes I will do this when I find myself in a situation in which I don't necessarily want to be. I may initially think, "Hmmm. What can I think about that's more interesting than being here?" And then I remember to practice going within and I do the "Breath-Heart-Mantra" game and I am immediately more calm, relaxed and content. My agitation releases. I am present. My perception is clear. I notice colors and life around me. And when I look at the people around me, I feel a connection and kinship, versus an irritation or dismissal. A peacefulness comes over my whole being and I create meaning and purpose simply being where I am.

There are other ways of connecting to your soul energy, like walking or sitting silently in nature, meditating, reading, writing and contemplating inspirational words. Also, dancing or listening to a beautiful piece of music can open the space for that soul connection. Opening to the soul connection is a vital step in discovering your true purpose.

> *"Everyone has been made for some particular work,*
> *and the desire for that work has been put into every heart."*
> —Rumi, Persian Poet

True Purpose

Many teachers and writers share their thoughts on the purpose of life. Thomas Merton, contemplative writer, says the whole purpose of life is to live by love. I would agree with that—love of self, love of others, love of all that exists. Eckhart Tolle, spiritual teacher and writer, says that our highest purpose is to bring the power of presence into the world. I can agree with that as well (see the "going within" section above). And yet, as we are cultivating our ability to live by love and bring the power of presence into the world, most of us must do something that requires us to put our ego (body and personality) into action. In other words, we must choose how to use our time while on this earth.

Zukav says that the purpose of our being is authentic empowerment, which he describes as "the alignment of the personality with the soul." Bingo! That is exactly what we are aiming for in discovering our true purpose—that precise place where the ego meets the energy of its own soul.

A crucial moment for me in my search for my own life's purpose was when I found Tim Kelley's True Purpose® work in the summer of 2008. This work taught me a methodology that has had a major impact in my life and the lives of many. Kelley explains that your soul already knows your purpose and that it is your ego's job to discover it. The discovering is a series of processes where you eventually get clear, detailed answers about your unique purpose. The journey begins by scanning your life for clues. Use the following method to begin unraveling your purpose in life.

Purpose Hunting

Purpose Hunting, a term coined by Kelley, entails answering certain questions in order to reveal important pieces of the puzzle to your unique and true purpose. Though this initial exercise may not give you the exact details of your purpose, it will certainly steer you in the right direction and prepare you to begin some deeper soul work when you are ready. What you are looking for are the times in your life when your soul and your ego were in sync. On paper or on your computer, answer the following questions.

1. When in your life have you felt the most fulfilled, passionate or content? Write down three different times in your life when you felt one or more of the above states. It is best to trust whatever comes to your mind first. It is also best to avoid the more universal experiences like falling in love, getting married, having a baby and so forth. Find some specific, detailed moments or events. For example, "When I went skiing with my husband in Colorado" or "When I was alone in the cabin in New Mexico writing for 10 hours a day" or "When I was 15 and talking to the elderly man in church." You are searching for what it was you were doing when you felt fulfilled, passionate or content and who it was that you were being.

After you write down three instances, explore each of them deeper by asking yourself, "What about that experience made me feel fulfilled, passionate or content?" You may say, for example, "I felt fulfilled because I was connecting to the heart of another person." Now keep probing deeper by repeatedly answering the question, "And why is *that* important to me?" You are searching for the bottom line in each of these experiences. Keep asking yourself this question until you reach a clear stopping point.

2. What are you drawn to again and again? Write down two or three things that you have been continually drawn to throughout your life. It could be that you have been drawn again and again to acting or being with children or playing an instrument or designing a home or sharing spiritual knowledge or writing. Try not to judge what comes up. Just observe and write.

After making your list, once again explore *why* you are drawn to those particular things. What about them draws you? For example, if you are drawn again and again to dance in some form, what is it about dance that draws you? Is it the beauty of it? Is it the performing aspect of it? Is it the pure expression of it? What need does dance fulfill in you?

Why one person is drawn to dance may be very different from why another person is drawn to it.

3. If you knew you didn't have long to live, what would you spend your time doing? Make a list of how you would spend your time if you knew your time was limited. Would you spend more quality time with your loved ones? Would you visit a certain place? Would you make amends with someone toward whom you have held grievances? Would you find out your true purpose in life? Often, some real gems are discovered from answering this question.

An additional direction you may choose to take with this question is to ask yourself, "What is holding me back from doing these things *now*?" After you have answered the above questions, find the common threads throughout them. For this, I encourage you to invite someone to help you. It is easier for someone else to help you evaluate repeating patterns that run through your life. Together, you may discover recurring themes such as: expressing yourself through music, easing pain and suffering, helping others see possibilities, solving problems, committing to excellence, sharing higher knowledge, etc. The themes you discover will point you in the direction of knowing your true purpose in life. This information can assist you in aligning your dreams and goals with what most resonates with who you are.

The True Purpose methodology takes further steps to help you gain more detailed information about your purpose through what Kelley refers to as "direct methods." These methods, such as guided meditation, dream work, prayer and "active imagination," are about creating a direct line of communication between your ego and your soul and receiving direct information. For instructions on these methods and more, I recommend Kelley's book, *True Purpose: 12 Strategies for Discovering the Difference You Are Meant to Make,* published in 2009 by Transcendent Solutions Press. I also strongly encourage you to work with a trained True Purpose® coach to assist you in your exploration.

Living Your True Purpose

Once you become aware of your unique and true purpose, it is like having a precious gem placed in your hands—a gem that requires care, maintenance and continued nurturing. Your purpose is entrusted to you to carry out to the best of your ability. Trust that the world needs what you, and only you, are uniquely designed to offer. Even if it seems similar to what someone else is offering, it has never been expressed through your particular voice, your particular life experiences and stories, your particular ego, your particular soul.

American writer Daniel Pink said, "I think that this search for meaning and purpose spread throughout the population is one of the most important things going on today." It is how you express the truth of your soul that has the greatest impact on your own life and the lives of others. Whatever form that soul-searching takes for you, I encourage you to keep the channel to the voice of the soul open and discover and live your true purpose for the benefit of all humanity. Now is the time!

ERIN SARIKA DELANEY, MA, CDC
Dreams in Motion

*Change agent for inner and
outer transformation*

(502) 797-7681
erin@dreamsinmotioncoach.com
www.dreamsinmotioncoach.com

Certified Dream Coach® and licensed True Purpose Coach,™ Erin guides individuals and groups to find detailed clarity about their true purpose in life and the contribution they are designed to make. She is a speaker, coach and workshop leader, who helps people access their inner wisdom and set their highest dreams in motion.

Erin has been exploring the inner realm of purpose and following her dreams throughout her life. Her search has lead her in many directions—from working with children at Mother Teresa's day camps in the Bronx to teaching English to teens in Mexico City; from training with Gabrielle Roth in the 5Rhythms® dance in California to studying sacred ritual in Bali; from living at a meditation ashram in the Catskill Mountains to working on a farm in Southern France.

No matter where her path leads, her secret is to listen to the wisdom of the soul and follow the call of the heart.

Erin holds an MA in the Expressive Arts and taught dance and creative writing for over 15 years. She currently lives outside of Berkeley, California with her husband, filmmaker and artist Dionisio Ceballos and their daughter Emilia.

Living An Incredible Life Starts with a Vision

Collaborate with the Universe to Create, Clarify and Realize Yours

By Maura Cronin, CDC, LMP

"Even if you're on the right track, you'll be run over if you just sit there."
—Will Rogers, American humorist and showman

I am sure you can relate to the feeling of being in a quandary about your true path in life and the difficulties of getting back on track if you feel derailed. As reality, time, basic needs and social constructs bump up against our passions, freedom, inspiration, spirituality and truth, you can sometimes find it hard to keep to your vision or keep it in focus.

The process of creating a vision for your life, or defining a vision you already have more specifically, can be overwhelming, but making the effort to do so has many rewards. By finding a clear direction and supporting that with a solid strategy, you can begin to create graceful, forward movement in your life. Several simple, inspiring tools can help you through this process and you can integrate them into your daily practice to further enhance the manifestation of your vision.

In the practice of living your life with your personal vision as your beacon, you will radiate a passionate, empowered sense of purpose with awareness and intention. In calling out for the visionary part of you to awaken, shine and guide you, you will learn to listen deeply, believe and call forward others with a similar vision and path to co-create and manifest with you. You will acknowledge your doubts and strengthen your faith as you share and clarify your dreams and make plans of action. Daily alignment and relationships with your vision will become natural, joyful and fulfilling.

Identify and Align with Values and Soul Essence

"Be faithful in small things because it is in them that your strength lies."
—Mother Teresa, Catholic nun and
Nobel Peace Prize recipient

Vision is the picture in your mind of where you want to go and how you sense that path unfolding. Your desire to actualize what you want or need is the passion that fuels you. You must believe in what your vision stands for. Passion tells you what rings true for you.

Vision is your higher self showing you the way. Others may have well-intended ideas for you, but if you have no passion it may not be your dream, and if it is not your dream, how can vision align and guide you?

Does this path have value to you and is it aligned with your values? If you cannot see yourself taking steps toward this dream, it may be a great idea but doesn't resonate with the greater part of you. There must be faith and belief. You must be able to see yourself realizing your vision and believe in this vision; otherwise, it is merely a fantasy. You do not have to believe or have all of the information and details you need right now, but you must have faith and passion—these are essential. What is your passion? Tune in to kinesthetic sensations like the excitement you feel when using your hands with small, creative details, or the thrill you get from orchestrating a big group project. It may be a simple idea or feeling, or it may be a grandiose dream. The important part is to tap into the faith and passion that will fuel the vision. Spend a few minutes thinking about it and write down three or four sentences that describe it.

Check in with the level of passion you have for your vision. Give it a rating between 1 and 10, with 10 meaning you are on fire with desire and 1 meaning your vision is flat and dull. If your vision isn't truly your heart's desire, your passion level will not be very high. Your inspiration and heart will not fully be there. Taking the steps to implement plans that move you closer to your vision will not feel completely right.

Imagine the power behind an idea that has been nurtured with faith and belief! The passion that can arise from that initial spark of conviction can be unstoppable. I quoted the Catholic nun, Mother Teresa, at the beginning of this section. She was a woman who had a passionate vision of tending to poor and dying people in the streets of Calcutta, India. Her vision grew to become an international order of nuns dedicated to helping the poor and disenfranchised in countries around the world. Did she envision receiving the Nobel Peace Prize? Probably not. It was icing on the cake and a result of her pure passion for the plight of the poor.

What is your vision? Draw, make a collage, snap a picture or write a song about what your vision looks like. Keep this image or inspiration where you can see it daily.

Steps to Manifest Your Vision

> *"The world stands aside to let anyone pass*
> *who knows where he is going."*
> —David Starr Jordan, American scientist and educator

Acknowledge the voice of the doubter and get your "self" out of the way. Doubt will sometimes keep you safe, but when it comes to your vision and dreams, your doubts can compromise your actions and squelch your inspiration. The ego mind feeds fear—yours, others' and that of the collective, and it can be suppressive when it gets out of control. It can kill every great idea with, "What if I can't?" or "I don't have enough _____ (money, education, and so on)." It is time to choose to believe in you and in your vision.

Create a vision that moves you. No matter how big, how simple or how silly your dream, begin to invite a strong feeling of faith in to drive your vision. Your first instinct is often the voice or action of the visionary. Trust this and respond before doubt can dampen it.

1. Close your eyes and center yourself.

2. Invite passion into your heart.

3. See your vision in your mind and anchor it, breathing deeply.

4. Deepen this vision by asking, "And?" and allowing for a stronger sense to come through. Maybe you will hear or feel or see more details.

5. Allow and open to the greater part of yourself and let more of the Universe feed your vision.

6. Notice when your mind questions or criticizes and ask it to step aside for now, that you are doing some visualization work and cannot be disturbed. Be clear about this. Be firm. You may only last a moment before the ego tells you this is silly or that you cannot do this simple exercise. The key is to push aside any thoughts or feelings that question, talk you out of the idea or dismiss it. Acknowledging the mind and the doubter keeps it satisfied and then you can choose to not focus any energy on it now.

Connect outward intention inward. We hear the word *intention* often these days, especially in the metaphysical and spiritual arena. We often think of the word *intention* as an active process outward; something we can manifest out there for ourselves. The prefix "in," however, is essential to visualize as is "tend to." Connecting your outward intention inward at its origination makes it that much more powerful with a clear connection to self and source. Taking a simple thought of something intended and bringing the senses into our heart and then outward makes the vision much more powerful and speeds its manifestation.

Years ago, my massage/craniosacral practice in Seattle was full, and I decided the office space ought to be utilized on my days off, Monday and Tuesday. I put out the intention for a practitioner who wanted to work on my days off. I went deeper with the vision and realized I really wanted a colleague with whom I could relate professionally and spiritually. Monday morning, Chuck, a Rolfer, appeared at my front door and asked if I had space available for Monday and Tuesday. He quickly became a friend and a professional with whom I teach and exchange treatments, techniques and clients to this day, a decade later.

You can learn to intend with your full senses, not solely with how you see your vision occurring, although "seeing" may be the primary way in which some people visualize and that, in itself, is very powerful. You may take it deeper, with greater clarity, by asking a few questions:

• How does this intention feel?

• Does it invoke a smell or a sense of feeling like chills, relaxation or deep emotion?

• Can this vision become more alive as I identify more specifically the root and details of it?

• Identify the "why." Because you deserve it? For your children? Because it was always your dream?

Close your eyes and try it. Intend something simple. Give it a color, some vibration, a movement. From where does it originate? How does it want to move? Can you feel it stirring, coming to life? Does it have "tension," a charge? Capture your deeper vision by writing it down.

> *"When I'm trusting and being myself... everything in my life reflects this by falling into place easily, often miraculously."*
> —Shakti Gawain, American author

Practice the path as the goal. The path is not always a direct one and for many, the path is the goal, especially if you hold spirituality as one of your values. The joy that comes from cultivating kindness, compassion and awareness on the path as a means to remain connected to vision and values is a treasure. Doors will open to worlds you could not imagine, and that sense of expansion can be fun. Awareness and a well-developed spiritual path can be brought into any arena and applied toward goals.

Before the vision even comes into thought form, the intention becomes part of our vibration. Close your eyes and connect deeply to the happiness you feel from your vision. It is important that you really feel the joy. This practice manages the voice of "I'll be happy when my dream comes true." Manifesting in the non-physical will enliven passion, deepen faith and align the vibration in your energetic field.

Ask for guidance in the vision process. Ask is a key word. You have angels and guides surrounding you, but you need to ask them for help. They have special gifts to help you bring forward your true vision.

One day in my meditation practice, I demanded that my guides reveal my true purpose to me. Within the month, I became part of a community of healers facilitating a retreat for regenerative brain function for some of the most influential leaders, performers, doctors, speakers and thinkers in our day. They came to us! This was expansion of my path in a way I could not have imagined. It came about because I was firm in my intention, open to greater possibility and stood from a place of gratitude. I asked firmly but with great humility and surrender.

It is said that the Universe does not acknowledge the word "No." It can only respond in these three ways:

- Not just yet. This is where asking and surrendering, or letting go with faith are essential. Taking active steps toward your vision can help things align more quickly, and surrender is key.
- Here's something better!
- Yes!

Journal to allow the creative flow to flourish. I recommend a journaling practice if you do not already have one, and setting an intention to focus on your vision. Allow the words to flow. If writing is not something you enjoy, make a vision board, draw, play music or paint—choose something that moves you and allows your vision to develop more clearly.

I have looked back into some of my journals of years past and found several clear examples where I had written down a goal or had been working out the details of a vision. At the time I had no idea that those dreams would actually become a reality or that getting the dream out of my head was a crucial step in the actualizing process!

Sometimes old, trapped, uncomfortable emotions may arise and express themselves through the vehicle you choose. Ask for the beliefs that limit you to come up, so you can process and shift them.

A coaching client of mine, Marilyn, was working on her intention for the next phase of her life. Through a series of self-discoveries, a completely new palette for her life's direction appeared. She recognized her limiting beliefs and her doubt, moved it aside and put out her intention to serve as an ordained minister. Requests for her services appeared and she responded with enthusiasm and passion. She felt valued and had a completely new sense of purpose that was in alignment with her faith, values, intention, spirituality, community and purpose. When we find our soul responding to something with passion and clarity, we must pay attention and take steps in response.

> *"Go confidently in the direction of your dreams.*
> *Live the life you've imagined."*
> —Henry David Thoreau, American author

Respond and actively create openings. A word, name, piece of information, or message can surprise us. The Universe works in mysterious ways, and wisdom and connection often come from some of the most unsuspected places. These are messages that source has heard and supports our vision. Remain open, listen and respond. Ask for one opportunity to manifest a confirmation of your vision tomorrow, and then start to cultivate the practice daily.

Vision with Purpose, Being and Presence of Alignment

You probably have had the experience of being in alignment with your vision, and it felt great! However, if you have lost that connection to purpose, try volunteering, it is a wonderful way to make a difference, recalibrate and examine purpose. When you are in service, you are aligned with something greater than you are, you make people feel inspired and at peace. They are drawn to you, sometimes unaware as to why or where there is an attraction. For more about volunteering, see Michele Rastovich's chapter, *Give a Little—Get a Lot,* on page 183.

> *"I've learned that people will forget what you said,*
> *people will forget what you did,*
> *but people will never forget how you made them feel."*
> —Dr. Maya Angelou, American poet, author and educator

Embrace these practices with confidence, compassion, faith and trust in using your vision as a guide. Acknowledge any doubts when they come up, but choose to move in the direction of your vision. Create a plan of action that you write down and share with another person. Break down steps into actions you can implement today, this week or within the month.

Dream big, start small, take the steps, and collaborate with the Universe to create and realize your vision. Surrender with faith, you have asked for this. Get started right now. Pull out a note pad and write down three steps you will take now to visualize your passion and bring it to reality.

MAURA CRONIN, CDC, LMP
Visionary Craniosacral Therapist
and Wellness Coach

(978) 525-3333
info@mauracronin.com
www.mauracronin.com

Maura Cronin weaves a unique blend of gifts, vision and presence into her being, her life evolution, and her healing and coaching practices. Years of extensive training and practice in diverse modalities have allowed her the opportunity to work closely with infants and children, women in labor, working professionals, the elderly and people from all walks of life. People come to Maura with dis-ease and discomfort in their physical and/or emotional bodies and she helps them reconnect with their core rhythm, true purpose and higher self with abundance and joy.

She has a rapidly growing and successful bi-coastal practice in Seattle; San Francisco; Los Angeles; Portland, Maine; Boston and Washington, D.C. Maura is a certified Visionary Craniosacral and Pediatric Craniosacral Practitioner and utilizes Visceral Manipulation, Developmental Movement,™ Hatha Yoga, kinesiology and massage therapies in her practice. She is also an Herbalist, Certified Dream Coach,® trained True Purpose Coach,® and Wellness Coach. She is a world traveler, artist and sharer of wisdom, and remains committed to her life's work of serving as a catalyst for "evolving higher purpose" with compassion, acceptance and inspiration.

Goal Setting
Charting Your Path to Success
By Jan McDonough, CDC, CDCGL, CEL, WABC

"Responsibility and initiative are tools that proactive people use to make things happen. Proactive people do not allow themselves to become victims of circumstance, instead they cause action!"

No matter what business you are in, or where you are in life, you can either wander aimlessly, simply reacting to whatever circumstances you encounter, or you can choose to chart your own course and determine your destination of success. Truly successful people understand that goals are simply dreams with a deadline. They visualize what they want, and then take specific actions to make those dreams a reality. They continue to inspire themselves by keeping a list of the benefits that will result by attaining their goals. They gauge their success by their actions, not by results. The results will come when they continue the actions. The focus on actions will create new habits that will empower you to a more incredible life. Here are the simple, yet profound, ways to create your own path to success.

Develop Your "Road Map"—
Start with the Destination in Mind

The road map helps you determine where you want to go. It is important to take the time to plan your journey so you don't "crash." One bit of caution as you prepare your map is to remember that sometimes it's easy to get so focused on the outcome that you forget to plan the steps that are needed along the way. Writing down steps toward your goal is another way of tracking your progress. It is especially important to write down your long-term goals. Long-term goals are not immediate goals; they are those you achieve over a period of time. Create a one-year goal, a five-year goal and a ten-year goal. Cross off each step as you achieve it for a greater sense of accomplishment. Consistency will lead toward simplicity, time-saving, credibility and integrity. Taking time to chart your course will mean so much toward supporting your self-confidence and helping you know when you have arrived.

As you begin to develop your road map, consider bringing along a guide as you set out on your journey. When you have a guide, you are provided effective direction to stay on the right path, establish your accountability and evaluate your progress. I strongly encourage you to get one of the following:

A mentor. This is a person who is looking out for your best interest, someone who has "been there, done that" and brings a wealth of knowledge and experience to the table. They have likely made all the wrong turns and ventured off the beaten path enough times to save you wear and tear. They will support and encourage you while you are working toward your goal. For example, if working on a weight goal, you may want a nutritionist as your mentor to make sure you are eating properly.

A coach. Someone who functions in this capacity can help guide you in the appropriate direction as you work toward your goal. You will want to check in with your coach to evaluate whether you are staying the course. Coaches are trained to help others succeed in life. Your coach will ask you questions and help you integrate everyday tools to move you toward your goal, providing you with a solid support system. Your coach's agenda is to assist you in accomplishing your goals—nothing more, nothing less.

An accountability partner or peer coach. This person can make a huge difference. This would be someone you check in with on a regular basis—weekly or monthly—to discuss the progress that has been made. It is a great way to re-focus and measure your progress as you move to the next step.

A mastermind group. This is a group of people with similar goals or values. Groups such as these can be very helpful in delivering other viewpoints. Sometimes the greatest results come from brainstorming with others. When we have a group whose members are trustworthy and committed to each other and who openly share their thoughts and ideas, we can all come away with greater benefits. Mastermind groups are known for creating synergy among group members.

Evaluate which of these guides fits your needs best. Do you think a mentor, a coach, an accountability partner or a mastermind group will best suit you? What do you need to put in place to have this support?

Once you have a guide or support system in place, you can begin to formulate your route. Be sure to look for:

Mile Markers—Short-term, Long-term, Personal and Professional

Break your journey down into milestones that you can easily achieve. Just as we pass mile markers along the road, we have measurable distances that allow us to track our progress. I like to use a graph that I color in as I move toward my goal. Others like to use thermometers. Create a visual that allows you to recognize forward progress toward your goal. We identify small achievements along the way, just as we would stop in cities on the way to our destination. When you take the time to break up the trip into segments, the anticipation becomes greater along the way.

Billboards and exit signs are tools to keep you alert to the messages provided to you while you are on your path. The billboards might supply information on resources to assist you in working toward your goal. Not all billboards are meant for you. Not every exit is for you either; however, taking an exit may allow you a break to re-group. Pay attention to every sign, as many will continue to provide direction. Some of the signs and exits you may encounter are:

Roadside assistance (education). Learn everything you can about the goal you have chosen to work toward. You may choose to do a search on the Internet for information. You may just need to observe. You may need to go to the local library to research in greater depth. Ask yourself questions. What is required? By when do I want to accomplish this? How will I know when I have achieved this goal?

Gas stations (power boosters). At times, particularly on long-term goals, it is important to take a break to sharpen your saw. You may need to refuel your excitement and energy toward obtaining your goal. A power booster may be a fabulous pair of pants you want to fit into. It may be a poster of the trip you are working to achieve. Your power booster is anything that energizes you about your goal. I like to listen to a favorite song. You may choose to drive to a specific location or share your progress with someone who will be excited with you. Maybe you have a picture that reminds you of what you are working toward.

Scenic overlooks (visualize and feel it). One way to view a scenic overlook is as a reminder to take the time to stop and enjoy the journey every now and then. Keep your mind clear and healthy while remembering to experience the trip. Scenic overlooks are an opportunity for you to see yourself successful or "act as if." When you want to achieve something intensely, try closing your eyes and just imagine yourself "there." Can you touch it, feel it, taste it and see it clearly? Can you review every detail in your mind? This will support you in maintaining a clear vision. Working out a specific level of concentration will help you visualize your true, deep down inside goal. This takes practice, just as learning to drive a car, but the payoff is well worth it. Take the time to really focus on "arriving" and hold that vision for those days when the road seems to go on forever. You will feel the transformation toward your goal starting to take hold.

We Have to Believe It Before We Can Achieve It

Mark Victor Hansen, author and speaker, refers to this method as the "Obi-Wan Approach." Do you remember Obi-Wan Kenobi from *Star Wars?* A scenic overlook is the place to put on your Jedi robe and start *thinking* "as if" and put your mind to work by asking your Higher Power to give you your heart's desire. Belief is the true source of power for thinking "as if." Words have a great deal of power, as well. Tell others where you are going and encourage them to be passengers on your journey. As you speak about your adventure, you will be *speaking* "as if." This creates conviction and is self-fulfilling. You will be building your enthusiasm every time you open your mouth! My favorite part of the *Star Wars* trilogy is in the second movie, *The Empire Strikes Back.* Luke Skywalker tells the Jedi Master Yoda that he is trying. Yoda replies, "Do or do not! There is no try!" Many people refer to *maybe* or *hoping.* Yoda knew the bottom line. You either make it happen or you don't. There is no in-between.

As you work with the "Obi-Wan Approach," you must speak only of success. Negative thoughts and words attract other negatives, such as our thoughts and feelings. The positive belief you have in yourself can be the difference between success and failure. Your belief system is a valuable tool for this goal setting process. Belief is a state or habit of mind in which trust or confidence is placed in some person or thing. We have to believe it before we can achieve it. Absorb that belief and keep it close to your heart. Revisit your belief often to keep it fresh and solid. Ask others to support your belief for extra encouragement. Remember that a true scenic overlook is a place of beauty and is awe-inspiring. Create your own gorgeous vistas as you move toward success.

What are your intentions for visualizing your goals? How will you keep the feeling alive along the way? What insights can you gain to strengthen belief in yourself achieving this goal?

The Rules of the Road

Make sure that you follow the rules of the road as you set out on your road to success. For example, you need to hold yourself accountable, or "Stay in Your Own Lane." When you work toward anything, it cannot come together unless you make the time to clock in and work at it. Goals cannot be achieved without your effort. There is no such thing as a magic wand. It is you and the activities you are willing to perform to get to the necessary locations. One step at a time will allow you to stay your course.

Some obstacles may just be bumps in the road. Take a step back, stop and review the situation. You will determine the intensity of the bump. At that point, you need to visit your resources: consult your map or stop at an information station. This would also be a great time to communicate with your coach or mentor. When you associate with the right people and use the right tools, you will find more joy and satisfaction during the journey.

Detours are occasionally unavoidable. Sometimes we just need to adapt to a different perspective. When we prepare or take an alternate route, we may get an even better result than we anticipated. This new perspective may even give you an energy boost you would not have had on the original path. It is important to stay open to all opportunities as we travel this journey.

My Personal Journey

Over the past 20-plus years in direct sales, it has become clear to me what goals are, and their purpose in my life. I set goals in a variety of areas such as finances, education, business, health, social, spiritual, travel and more. I have learned the hard way that there are many roads available to any given goal. The key is to find the best route for you.

I have found that regardless of the type of goal, the same strategies can be used and applied. To develop my road maps, I have used a process known as SMART goals. "SMART goal" was a term originated in 1981 by George T. Doran, who said "There's a SMART way to write management's goals and objectives." Arthur F. Miller and James A. Cunningham wrote about it in "How To Avoid Costly Job Mismatches," *Management Review,* November 1981, Volume 70, Issue 11.

S	–	Specific
M	–	Measurable
A	–	Attainable Action Steps
R	–	Relevant
T	–	Timely

Set specific goals. The more detailed you can be, the easier it is to break your goal down into mile markers. This allows you to more clearly see the possibilities of turning this goal into reality. The goal must be clear and defined to create the necessary steps toward the goal to show you the way.

Set measurable goals. Allow yourself to chart progress and measure your degree of success toward your specific goal. Knowing your progress along the way gives you opportunities for small celebrations. Achievements, big or small, can assist in boosting your confidence. These "mini celebrations" can go a long way toward building the inspiration and motivation to take the next steps.

Set attainable goals. Attainable goals are within reach; they are manageable. You have the ability to create the necessary action steps on your way to realizing your goal. If you set a goal that is not possible or within your reach, it is self-defeating and creates disappointment that can easily hold you back from future successes. You will want your goal to be a stretch, but not beyond reach. Too big a goal can deteriorate your self-confidence and cause you to move backward away from your goal.

Set relevant goals. This is the area where you want to make sure your goals are in alignment with where you are headed in life or in your career. Keep your goals relevant to allow you to create consistency in the appropriate direction toward your success.

Set time-specific goals. It is important to identify a specific time period or time span in which you will achieve this goal. Your goal must have a deadline for completion. At times, it can create urgency, increasing your energy level for completion. After all, a goal is nothing more than a *dream with a deadline.*

Here are a few examples of goals:

VERB/NOUN	MEASUREMENT	DATE
Read books	12	One a month
Lose weight	25 pounds	By October 31st
Become director	Next step	By conference
Have children	2	By age 40

As you can see by these examples, there is a detailed, measurable action that can realistically be reached by the time frame specified.

Let's face it—if you don't know where you are going, you will probably not end up where you want to be.

Think about what you really want.

1. Set a realistic goal—a dream with a deadline.

2. Have a plan—a road map, complete with all the stops along the way.

3. Take action—act on your plan daily, focus on what is important.

To show your commitment, write your goals down on paper. Consider making note cards with your destination clearly defined and placing them in places where you will frequently see them, maybe on the bathroom mirror, your visor in your car, on the refrigerator and in your wallet. The visual prompt of having this written goal in front of you is another tool in helping you stay the course.

I challenge you to see the importance of not only having a goal, but also making your goal a priority. Once you complete one goal—set another one. You want to have the vision of a goal so you can continue to have clarity of direction. I like to use my GPS to provide direction.

Goals—step-by-step path to where I want to be

Positive Attitude—creates resiliency and allows growth

Spirit of Service—reaching out to help others will return with rewards to me

You will discover that it is one thing to say your goal; it is another to live your mission daily. There are no secrets, there are only lessons learned. You decide your future that will determine your destiny.

Setting goals is *not* a one-time endeavor. Setting goals is a process, something you revisit on a regular basis. During this continuous review, you may find some adjustments are necessary to keep your goals relevant and important. Goal setting is much more than just wishing for something to happen. Unless you have taken the time to clearly identify what it is that you truly desire, any positive results will be diminished greatly.

Just as with choosing your next vacation destination, you don't just snap your fingers and appear in that location. It is a process of breaking down how you will get there. How long will the journey take? What is your target date?

I challenge you to start today by writing down your goal and creating your road map. Take control of your success, you are in the driver's seat and you are the only one in charge. You can have, do or be whatever you want, if you are willing to set goals and work toward them.

JAN MCDONOUGH, CDC, CDCGL, CEL, WABC
Attitude Adventures

Exploring the unlimited paths of possibilities

(763) 971-8583
jan@attitudeadventures.com
www.attitudeadventures.com

Jan is currently based in Minneapolis, Minnesota, and has been making a difference in the lives of others for more than 20 years. She has supported both men and women alike, from stay-at-home parents to career changers to established professionals. When her clients want more, she provides them with the tools and confidence that guide them on the path to making their dreams come true. Jan works with individuals and organizations. She has spoken to groups not only in the USA but also worldwide. Creating and executing action plans is Jan's way of empowering people to realize their potential and expand it for a higher-quality life.

Jan has earned multiple top honors from her direct sales company in the United States, North America and worldwide levels, as well as from the Direct Selling Women's Alliance (DSWA). She is well-respected within the profession. Jan is also a Certified Dream Coach® and Certified Group Leader through Dream Coach University.

Jan reaches out and connects with her audiences. She keeps her training fun, informative and interactive. You will be inspired and empowered by Jan's never-ending energy.

The Sweet Spot

Where the Law of Attraction
Meets the Law of Action

By Sheryl Eldene, MA, MBA, PCC

*T*here is a magical place on the strings of a tennis racket where the ball just bounces perfectly and a winning shot is created. Where is that sweet spot on your life? Where is the place where those ideas and dreams just bounce off and create your ideal life? Look around at what is in your life today. Did you know that what you see today is a result of what you attracted to yourself on the strings of your heart before today? Did you hit your dreams off the court, or over the net? Let's take a deeper look at the "Law of Attraction" strings, and see how to weave them in with your "Law of Action" strings to create the perfect sweet spot for your dreams.

> *"Whether you think you can, or you think you can't,*
> *you're right."*
> —Henry Ford, American automobile magnate

The Law of Attraction

In a nutshell, the Law of Attraction says that "Like attracts like." Reaching back in the collective wisdom, we can look thousands of years earlier to King Solomon from Proverbs 23:7 who said, "As a man thinketh in his heart, so is he." I hear you: "Pretty words, but what does that have to do with my run-down car, or my empty bank account, or my crying baby?"

A lot, actually. Remember a time when you had to go to a social event with your spouse's friends and you just knew it would be boring and tiring, and it usually turned out that way? Did you wonder why some of the other wives, who disliked football just as much as you, managed to enjoy the event? Or remember a different event when you were really looking forward to it, like going to your favorite spa, and that turned out wonderful. You know, I'll bet there were some customers that day that left the spa tired, angry, feeling used by the expense, and vowing never to return. It is easier to understand how your expectations shape your experience in circumstances such as these.

What I love most about living in this age is that, in our scientific pursuits, we are finding King Solomon to be accurate. We now understand that millions of packets of information enter our awareness every second. To remain sane, we filter out what is important for us through a part of the brain called the reticular activating system. Its job is to let in only those packets that we tell it are important to us. We do not need to know that a brown bird rather than a black bird is sitting on the wire above the intersection as we drive to work, so we do not see that. We do not need to know how many red Porsches are on the road, so we only notice cars around us that look like they may not stop at the stop sign.

Okay, what about that crying baby? When you hold your focus on how frustrated you are, guess what you get: more anxious moments. That is what your wonderful brain filter is providing. At this point, thinking "quiet baby, quiet" just seems a little loony, kind of out of touch with reality. Stay with me: using the Law of Attraction with the Law of Action really works. Let's walk through the process of how to do that.

Your Vision

The first step in any creation is deciding what you want to create.

Sounds simple, I know, but we will need a lot more specific details than "new car" to actually engage the Laws. What is your perfect vision for a car? What make and year is it? What color is it? What does it smell like? What do you hear when you are in this car? How do you physically feel sitting in the driver's seat? How do you feel emotionally? When you drive it, what do you see out the window? Are you on a road trip with it, or parking it near your work? Make your vision as specific and complete as possible. However you envision your life with this car, envision it with sounds, smells, tastes, feelings and pictures.

Try writing a "day in the life" script. Start with waking up, knowing that the car is in the garage waiting for you after your shower and breakfast, getting into it, driving out of the garage, parking it, returning to it after work or your meetings. Continue writing with as many details as you can make up all the way to the point when you return to your bed for a night of grateful sleep.

What is your vision for your life? Does it include a house with a white picket fence, a perfect life partner, the ability to ice skate gracefully on the lake? Pretend that while you sleep tonight, a miracle happens and you awake to your perfect life. What is the first thing you notice that is different? Notice what you *do* see, rather than what you *don't* see. From this list of life areas, what seems to catch your attention on that morning?

LIFE AREAS	
Family	Self Care
Career	Money
Education	Home
Romance	Social Life
Fun	Spirituality

Create and Use Affirmations

This is the step when you are re-programming that filtering part of your brain to work on behalf of your new vision. We also know it as the mysterious mind or the subconscious. There are several processes that I find helpful, depending on your own natural preferences.

Affirmations. When using affirmations, always state them in the present tense, with a date and an emotion. In our case, an affirmation could be, "It is January 5th and I am checking my bank account online. I just love finding new interest posted to my account and my savings growing easily. I know that my money is growing. I am rested, wearing my favorite shirt and I can smell dinner on its way. My favorite music is playing. Life is good."

To allow that affirmation to really become part of the way your brain functions, we will need to add a strong emotional memory. As a psychotherapist, I know that when a person is in a strong emotional state, it is the ideal time for them to create a new belief, whether that state is difficult (fear, anger) or pleasant (joy or pride). Think of a time in your life when you experienced a wonderful, strong emotion. I often remember when I got married or when I reached the top of Mt. Hood. I imagine the situation until I feel it, then I speak the affirmation and continue to feel the feeling. To be effective, the affirmation process is best done at the same time in the same place for 30 days in a row.

Vision board. The second process that I use a vision board. Your subconscious records and remembers in pictures. This, by the way, is why your affirmation must be positive. If you say, "I don't have a noisy, angry neighbor," since there isn't a picture of "don't," the picture emblazoned on your subconscious is—you guessed it—a noisy, angry neighbor! For your vision board, find pictures that represent your dreams: a picture of what you might be wearing, of what a friendly, quiet neighbor looks like, what the perfect friendly exchange looks like, what a peaceful neighborhood is—you get the idea. Place this vision board where you are likely to see it several times during the day. Drink in the joy and happiness represented there.

Prayer/meditation. The third process is prayer or meditation. If you have a prayer practice, know that gratitude is the only prayer. In *Conversations with God,* originally published by Putnam in 1996, Neal Donald Walsh talks about asking God for something. "Please God, I need to lose weight," and God says, "Absolutely, you got it, the experience of needing to lose weight." Instead, use, "Thank you God for this beautiful, flexible body, a gift from heaven" or whatever matches your own style of thanksgiving. If you have a meditation practice, sit, quiet your mind, and allow every cell of your body to rest in the state of being in that comfortable body as if it has already manifested for you. Just feel it wholly, if even for a few seconds.

Look for Evidence of Coming Success

Now it is up to God or the Universe. Your only job is to be your own search engine for evidence. Sometimes this is best done using a Gratitude Journal or an Evidence Journal. At the end of the day, record only those situations that match your vision.

- "From 2:00 until 2:10, Baby Jane was happy and quiet." If the only evidence you find is that precious ten minutes, celebrate it!

- "I saw two red Chevy Camaros today, I haven't seen one for years! See, my vision is on its way."

- "I found a new way to generate money today that will go directly into my savings. This is working."

- "I took the four dollars that I usually spend on a latte today, and put it in my savings jar. Woohoo, I'm getting this savings thing!"

The point here is that you find and record everything that matches your vision, no matter how small. Train your brain to find what is working, and you will find more and more of that. "As a man thinketh, so is he," and as you think and feel yourself happy and fulfilled, you do, in fact, experience happiness and fulfillment.

Now that the first half of the formula is complete—engaging the Law of Attraction—let's weave that together with the Law of Action and really release the "genie in the jar."

Law of Action

> *"Begin with the end in mind, put first things first."*
> —Dr. Stephen R. Covey, American author,
> *The 7 Habits of Highly Effective People*®

Jeane Dixon was a teacher who my mother loved back in the '50s. Dixon used to say, "Pray like everything depends on God, then act as if everything depends on you." My version of that wisdom comes from my navigation system. Since my car is a lovely metallic green color, I call her Lizzy. When I punch in the destination and just sit in the parking lot, *nothing happens*. When I start moving, Lizzy says to me, "Please proceed to the highlighted route, then the route guidance will start." Now, isn't that just something, a metallic green car teaching me about laws! We've done the first part of the instruction—now let's get moving toward that highlighted route.

Naming a Goal

In all project planning, the first step is to name a goal. To engage the Law of Attraction, we have set a specific goal, and we followed the SMART rules, as described on page 27 in Jan McDonough's chapter, *Goal Setting*.

"By January 5th, I have a lifestyle that provides for my health and happiness in my 150-pound body. I love this lifestyle and enjoy the thought that this is how I live. I stand ready to accept this or something better for the highest good of all concerned."

Create Action Steps

There is an art to creating action steps that respects both the desire to change as well as the desire to keep things the same. "What is the smallest step I can do now that moves me toward my goal of this new lifestyle of saving money regularly?" Here is where the weaving of the two laws is so powerful. When you have this open question hanging in the air, and you do your meditation, visioning or prayer, the next right step often just pops into your head. Take these suggestions from the Universe as evidence that the process is working, not as commandments from God on what *should* work. Try it out. If it works, that's great. If it doesn't, try something else. It's all good, it all leads to your goal. Just keep moving forward on the highlighted route, and I promise you, your internal navigation system will help with any course corrections necessary.

You decide if the action step you have created needs to be acted upon once, for several days in a row or for a couple of weeks. If that action step is to set an appointment with your doctor to be sure your baby is healthy, do that. Maybe your action step is to find a different coffee shop that provides a good latte for a dollar or two less. Maybe those steps include finding other owners of the car you want or taking a test drive in that car. When you are open, there is a deep wisdom that is alive within you and "miracles" do happen when you tap into that source. You may not have the entire project completely mapped out, but as you discover the next right steps, you will begin to get a hint about other steps you would like to try. Resist the temptation to try everything you hear about or think of. Remember, you are changing a pattern that has probably been in place for decades, and you want to make the change with ease and grace—one tiny step at a time.

Create a Schedule

When you have your action steps, add time stamps to them when possible. If one step is to set up a time with your doctor or nurse practitioner, write down on your calendar when you will have that appointment scheduled. If a step is to set up an automatic savings plan with your bank, put it on the calendar. Here's a word to the wise: Every time you promise your Self that you will act on your behalf and you follow through, your inner Self experiences love and affirmation. When you drop the ball, your inner Self experiences neglect, hurt and sadness, and you slip back a step on the self-esteem staircase. The only message that your deepest Self hears is the one you personally send when you follow through with your promises to yourself. Create a schedule and follow through. Your greater happiness and fulfillment depend on it.

Accountability Partner

Real change requires commitment, and although we would rather have it otherwise, commitments we make to others seem to get our attention more than our commitments to ourselves. We will use this awareness to add power to the action plan. Choose an accountability partner who knows your goal, knows your next action step and stands ready to ask how you are doing. This partner may be a life partner, a friend, a mastermind group, a coach or a counselor—anyone who agrees to connect with you weekly and hold your feet to the fire. Once you have selected this partner, schedule a regular, weekly check-in time.

Track Your Progress

Now, the only step remaining for the Law of Action is to track your progress in your Evidence Journal. Record specifically how many moments of peace you had on day one, day two, etc. When you are living in the trenches, it is difficult to notice progress, so this step is critical.

Also, be sure to celebrate these victories. Create your own list of celebration ideas, including anything from a simple cup of celebration tea to a day at the spa. You decide what feels like a just reward for the steps of the journey. It is so easy to get engaged in action steps and perfectionism that acknowledging the accomplishment of the small steps gets ignored.

The Sweet, Sweet Spot

Follow these steps to find your own "sweet spot."

1. Create your vision and write a SMART goal.

2. Take steps to create a new thought pattern and a newly-felt sense of that goal using affirmations, vision boards, prayer and meditation.

3. Create action steps with completion dates and follow-through.

4. Keep an Evidence Journal of whatever part of your vision you see present today.

5. Give thanks and celebrate yourself, your process and the gift from God or the Universe for your manifestation.

Now you have a full set of strings on which to play your heart song. Enjoy, and let me know how it's going for you!

SHERYL ELDENE, MA, MBA, PCC
On Purpose Living Center

*Where the Law of Attraction
meets the Law of Action*

(503) 297-8805
sheryl@oplcenter.com
www.oplcenter.com

Sheryl Eldene is a certified life coach as well as a licensed counselor. She studied with Dr. Martin Seligman, the Father of Positive Psychology, and was awarded the standing of Certified Authentic Happiness Coach. As a licensed counselor, she specializes in supporting women through recovery from trauma, and living through life-threatening health diagnoses. She is one of ten Premier Coaches for the eWomen Network,™ a national organization of over 45,000 members. Since establishing the On Purpose Living Center in 1995, she has helped thousands move toward their shining, successful, thriving selves.

Sheryl is a lively and engaging speaker, and part of her ongoing mission is to inspire others toward full use of their innate gifts—both at work and at home. She helps people walk away with a better understanding of how to tap into their own strengths and the strengths of the people around them, as well as their own unique connection to the organizations of which they are a part.

Sheryl invites her clients to explore the magic of being deeply heard and seen as they discover the power of knowing and manifesting exactly what works for them. She delights in helping them turn their dreams into *this* year's realities.

Believe in Yourself!

You Have the Power to
Create the Life You Want

By Mary Jones

Goose bumps. They are what life should be filled with. They are the greatest gift you can give yourself on a regular basis. For me, they have always signified that I was truly living and steering my life, not just being. Goose bumps come from dreaming big and living big. There is no greater or more inspiring feeling than the exhilarating rush you get when you can see, taste and practically feel a dream coming true.

Back in 2002, I made a career change, leaving the corporate recruiting firm that I had owned for many years to begin a radio talk show. The show is a positive look at everyday life. I wanted to come up with a signature sign-off to my daily show that had significance to me and would hopefully begin to have meaning for my listeners. I instantly knew what I was going to use. Three words that for me, were powerful. Three words that I felt were life-altering and confidence-building. *Believe in yourself.* Those words gave me goose bumps.

When was the last time you created a goose bump moment for yourself? If it hasn't been recently, your inner belief and self-confidence might be keeping you from all that you deserve and can achieve in life—and from getting your goose bumps.

How do you get goose bumps?

You Have More Control Than You Might Think

It is true. You have a lot more control over your life than you might realize. That, in and of itself, is a thoroughly powerful thought. *It is up to you, not the external world, to create and realize the life you want.* Pause for a moment, re-read and ponder that sentence. Have you truly believed and embraced that throughout your life? If not—start now.

The beauty of having control over our lives is that we do not need to depend on others or outside factors for our success and happiness. As I am sure you have heard before, while we cannot control everything that happens to us, we can control our reactions to those things. And those reactions are what set us on a path of fulfillment—or heartache. It is a choice. An inner belief in yourself helps you choose the right path.

> *"They can do all because they think they can."*
> —Virgil, Roman poet

Self-Confidence Can Be Developed

You can increase your self-confidence. It is up to you. Whether you need a boost from low self-esteem or from a temporary setback, you have all the power you need to make it happen—everyone does. You just need the will to make it happen. Now, *that* is worthy of a goose bump.

One of the best ways to change the way you feel about yourself is to recognize that it is the difference between having a positive and negative mind set. It does not need to be any more complicated than that. There is an almost instant transformation once you adopt a positive thought and behavior pattern. You are more in control. The world is more exciting. Your life improves.

"No one can make you feel inferior without your consent."
—Eleanor Roosevelt, former First Lady of the United States

I Challenge You!

Over the years, I have developed concise tips and reminders to get and keep me on course with my outlook on life and on pursuing my dreams. They are specific and practical. I have incorporated them into my radio show as *Monthly Challenges* that my listeners and I embark on together. I invite you—no, challenge you—to join us in taking on these challenges for yourself. You will be surprised at the positive impact on your daily life.

What or who motivates you? We all have experiences or people in our lives that can serve as motivating factors. Figure out yours. It may be a family member, school mentor or historical figure about whom you have read who gives you the model or inspiration. My mother, who graduated from college in 1939, was one of the few young women at that time to major in math and chemistry. She stepped outside the norm. I have reminded myself of that many times during my life and it has served as a source of inspiration to do the same. Identify the motivators in your life and hold them close to you—they are the sources of your dreams.

Let go of self-limitations. If you have labels from your past that inhibit you, choose to let them go. Many of us have them, leftover from childhood, teachers and parents. Do not let them define you one minute longer. Think about them honestly. Question their accuracy. As a young girl, a close friend of mine was often told by her parents and older siblings that she was clumsy. As a result, she shied away from physical activities, dancing and gym classes. In her early thirties, with encouragement from friends, she bought her first pair of sneakers in years and began jogging with a co-worker. She loved it. Though she still heard the "clumsy" word in her mind, she ran past it. She joined a jogging club, lost weight, successfully ran two marathons and her confidence soared. Take back control of your inner critic. You can do it by beginning to hear your inner voice giving you only positive feedback. When you hear a self-limiting thought in your mind, instantly tune it out and replace it with something affirming. With just a bit of practice, you can begin to use your inner critic's power to your benefit, not detriment.

Look at your strengths and weaknesses. You do realize that you have weaknesses? Everyone does. Do not pretend that you do not have weaknesses, or hope that no one will discover them. The key is to acknowledge what they are and use that knowledge to your advantage. For example, do not choose a career that requires skill in an area that is a weakness. More importantly, do not allow your weaknesses to create a less-than-perfect image of yourself, or to drive you to be anything that you feel bad about. Embrace your weaknesses. Laugh at them. Do not let them undercut your self-confidence. Do not be someone who wastes precious energy or time feeling inadequate because of them.

Now for the fun part—working with your strengths. What could be more exciting than focusing on those attributes at which you excel and get you jazzed? Isn't it totally uplifting to think about them, and ponder all the places they can take you? To get you started, ask yourself this question: "What do I enjoy?" We don't fail at things that we enjoy doing. I have asked a lot of people about the times in their lives when they experienced what they perceived to be failures. Invariably, those times were spent involved in activities or jobs that they didn't enjoy. If you identify your strengths and areas of passion, and revolve your life and career around them, you will have success. It really is that simple—and exciting!

Become comfortable thinking and talking about what you like about yourself. Make a list and refer to it often. Women seem to struggle with this a bit more than men. Many women innately feel that it is cocky or arrogant to speak about themselves in positive terms. Nonsense! Start by giving yourself three compliments daily. Think about what you have been complimented on over your lifetime, and again, do not overlook your physical attributes. Do you remember the first time you received a compliment about your appearance? What specifically was said? I remember mine. While there may have been previous ones, I specifically remember a man commenting on my "nice calves." I found it funny at the time to even notice a person's calves. But a compliment is a compliment. We sometimes have a hard time seeing or believing attributes in ourselves that others see easily. You can probably quickly list what you perceive to be your weaknesses and downsides. Most women can. Become as comfortable talking about your strengths and assets. If you struggle with this, ask your good friends, siblings or spouse what positive aspects of your personality, character or appearance they notice. Undoubtedly you will be surprised and elated to discover how others view you. It will be a fun and eye-opening exercise.

Surround yourself with positive and supportive people. Take an inventory of those in your immediate support system. Are they the type of people you aspire to become? It is more significant than you may realize. If you are surrounded by negativity, cynicism or people who thrive on personal drama, those qualities will infiltrate your attitude and energy regularly. Be around cheerful people, and be protective and selfish about those with whom you share your life.

Take yourself and life less seriously. Life is intended to be celebrated and enjoyed. Good self-esteem will allow you to laugh at yourself. You will have an easier time admitting mistakes and will not feel the need to be defensive or blame others. Do not worry about embarrassing yourself or looking foolish. I actually believe that looking silly should be a goal, something of which you can be proud. It indicates that you have a lighthearted sense of yourself, a good level of confidence and a willingness to take risks and embrace life. I say, go for it.

Dream big! Figure out what you really want to create for your life. It may seem silly to say, but you need to have a dream before your dream can come true. Many people do not feel that they deserve to live a dream-filled life. They feel their lot in life is to simply muddle through. Not so. Open yourself up to the possibilities awaiting you. Dream big—and go for it.

Care less what others think. This can be a tough one, but for a moment, imagine not being affected by criticisms and unkind comments that might be said about you. It feels rather liberating and exhilarating, right? There are certainly people in your life whose opinions you want to be concerned with—your spouse or boss, for example. But consider the drain on your energy and confidence that others' unwanted comments create. Keep in mind that what matters is what you think about yourself.

What makes you smile on a daily basis? Ask yourself this question. The answer may or may not surprise you, but it will give you specific insight into the things in your life that make you happy and from which you can derive strength—and increase your self-confidence.

Figure out what you love and surround yourself with it. A big part of how we feel about ourselves is how we feel about our surroundings. Whether it is your home, office or activities, know what warms your heart and puts a smile on your face. Recognize that you deserve to have a beautiful environment that will relax, comfort and rejuvenate you.

Do not be intimidated by anyone or anything. Sounds tough? It does not need to be. Make a habit of approaching situations and people from a positive perspective. Expect positive outcomes, and you will get more of them. One truly simple trick is to act confident, even if you are not feeling it. Research shows that your body will begin to feel the way it is acting, so if you act self-assured you will soon begin to feel it. For your next job interview, business presentation or networking event, act confident. It is your choice, after all.

Be happy for other people's successes. Be truly happy. Even for those you don't feel deserve it. By opening up your heart and spirit to celebrating others' victories and accomplishments, you will be drawing that same energy into your life. And you will be freeing yourself of those unhealthy resentments that create nothing but negativity for you. Give yourself the gift of being happy for others.

> *"You can't help someone get up a hill without getting closer to the top yourself."*
> —General H. Norman Schwarzkopf, U.S. Army Officer

Be in a good mood—for no reason. We feel better, in general, when we are in good moods. For whatever reason, that is true. We take on more challenges and live with more gusto when our mood is high. However, you do not need to wait for a reason to be in a good mood, as many people do. While a call from a friend, praise from your boss or thoughts of upcoming weekend plans can certainly boost your overall feeling of well-being, how about bringing that same feeling into your daily life for no specific reason. It is something you have the power to do, and you will reap the benefits.

I developed a tool a few years ago that can help. This *Happiness Meter* can diffuse feelings of stress, sadness, etc., before they escalate. If these emotions go unaddressed, they build. Your momentary bad mood or negative emotion can continue for hours, days and weeks, becoming a part of your daily life—this is not necessary. At any point during your day, ask yourself, "How happy am I feeling right now?" Do not focus on how you were feeling yesterday or how you hope to feel tomorrow, but right now. On a scale of 1–5, with 5 being the highest, assign a number to your level of happiness at that moment: 1 = despondent, 2 = stressed/frazzled, 3 = content, 4 = pretty darn happy and 5 = ecstatic. If you relate better to visual images than words: 1 = a black cloud over you, 2 = your hair standing on end, 3 = a comfy chair, 4 = a smiley face, and 5 = you doing a cartwheel.

1. Despondent 3. Content 5. Ecstatic

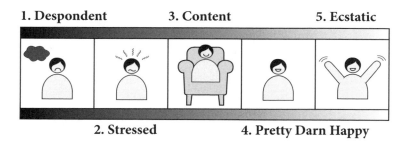

2. Stressed 4. Pretty Darn Happy

If you peg yourself at a 2, for example, have an arsenal of things that you can instantly do anywhere that will raise your number to a 3. You can absolutely raise your *Happiness Meter* number at any time. Remember, you have more control over your life than you may realize. Think of what in your life makes you happy—develop a list. Some suggestions: think of your dog, cat, child or spouse. Take five deep breaths, deep into your diaphragm. Play your favorite song. Read a page from a favorite book. Figure out what works for you— it's different for everyone. Use this simple technique to elevate your mood and reduce your stress. It's simple and it works.

There they are—my guideposts to follow on your road to a happier, more confident you. Live the life you deserve. Celebrate the future and the success that you can create. Your inner belief gives you full control and the ability to give yourself goose bumps.

MARY JONES
The Mary Jones Show

Believe in yourself!

(860) 748-1918
mary@maryjonesshow.com
www.maryjonesshow.com

"Believe in yourself" is Mary's motto; it's a message she's been spreading for 10 years. Mary's message is that attitude underlies all our activities. All of your successes and failures spring from your attitude about yourself. Attitude defines your happiness and your interactions with others in relationships and your life's work. Your joys, ambitions and your attractiveness as a person people want to be with, all come from what you feel about yourself as a person.

Mary hosts a positive, engaging and woman-oriented talk show on WDRC-AM in Hartford, CT and its three affiliate radio stations, and two weekly features on television. Her show has evolved into a strong community of listeners who share conversation and insights into issues of everyday life. Her audiences talk about everything connected to home, health and heart. She has translated these topics into frequent convention and luncheon appearances and into her popular bimonthly *Girls Night Out* events throughout Connecticut.

She has taken "believe in yourself" to heart throughout her career by re-inventing herself and following her dreams, which have moved her from social work to owning a corporate recruiting firm and then on to media. Mary is a contributing author in *The Power of Persistence* which reached #1 in Amazon's self-improvement category.

Think Your Way to Success, Health and Happiness
What You Think Does Matter
By Carol Stanley

*H*ave you ever felt so stressed you wanted to run away or put your head in the sand like an ostrich attempting to make the world go away? I am sure you have. I imagine you have also experienced great happiness, love and elation and how good that feels. There is a vast difference in the two as to how you feel all over, physically, mentally, spiritually and certainly emotionally.

How do you feel physically and emotionally when you are stressed and want to run away? How do you feel physically and emotionally when you are experiencing love and happiness or elation and success? How and what you think in any situation influences your emotions, attitudes and body responses, thus your health and happiness and ultimately, your behavior.

I want you to experience on a regular basis the good thoughts and emotions of love, joy, success and health. There is great good waiting for you in understanding and putting healthy thinking into practice.

"As a person thinks so he or she is."

What Lies Behind the Windows of the Mind?

According to Dr. Caroline Leaf, neuroscience researcher, *the brain* and *thoughts* lie behind the windows of your mind. She states that science and research now agree:

- The body-mind connection is real and is a critical key to physical, mental and emotional wellness.

- How and what you think are keys to successful, happy, stress-free living.

- Thoughts create electrical-chemical reactions from the brain to the body.

- Thoughts are intimately linked to emotions and affect your attitudes, body and behaviors.

- Eighty-seven percent of all illnesses can be attributed to thought life.

- Only thirteen percent of all illnesses can be attributed to diet, genetics and environment.

- Toxic thinking produces toxic emotions which are linked to chronic diseases like migraines, hypertension, strokes, cancer, skin problems, diabetes, infections and allergies—to name a few.

Science and research also agree that you can think yourself clever, calm, healthy, out of anxiety, out of bitterness and resentment, into forgiveness, into control of your emotions and out of stress!

Every thought is electrically and chemically attached to an emotion. No thought is void of an emotion attached to it. They are inseparable. The progression is like this:

- Thoughts stimulate emotions.
- Emotions result in attitudes.
- Attitudes produce behavior and bodily reactions.

Negative, destructive thinking is electrochemically attached to destructive emotions, producing negative destructive attitudes and behaviors, creating destructive electrochemical reactions in the body. As a result, you do not feel well, and you are set up to become very ill.

In the same way, positive rejuvenated thinking produces good attitudes, physical feelings and behaviors. Depending on the quality of the thought and emotion you choose to entertain, you can be helped or harmed by their corresponding chemicals to your brain and body. According to Dr. Candace Pert, a pioneering neuroscientist, emotions and their biological components establish the crucial link between the mind and the body. She calls these bio-chemicals "molecules of emotions." These molecules of emotions create copies of your thought life and corresponding emotions and carry the information to your whole body, potentially changing cellular structure on the outside and even your DNA on the inside.

"Both Sides Now"

The old song—*Both Sides, Now* (1969) Reprise Records, sung by Joni Mitchell—is true of the brain. The brain has distinct left and right hemispheres. Make two fists and hold them side by side with thumbs on top. This represents the two hemispheres of your brain in similar shape and size. Men's brains are usually larger than women's brains. Women's brains are just more compact.

The left hemisphere was once thought to be responsible for linear, logical and analytic functions, while the right hemisphere was thought to be your creative, artsy side where rhythm and color lived. These are now known to be false assumptions. We used to think you used each side separately for different functions.

The truth is the brain has mirror neurons in both sides and the two sides must work together rather than in separate functions. You must use *both sides* together, the left side seeing the details, then the big picture, while the right side sees the big picture, then the details.

Do you like puzzles? A puzzle is a great representation of how the brain must work together to be healthy. The puzzle pieces are the necessary details of the overall big picture. The left side of your brain sees the details or pieces first and how they fit into and create a big picture. The right side sees the big picture first and then the details, or that there are detailed pieces to be fitted into the big picture.

Math could seem too difficult if you were not taught to think with both sides of your brain at once. Two times two equals four. The left side of your brain sees the details of two times two, and that it is equal to four, the big picture. The right side of your brain sees four as the big picture, but also must see how the details of two groups of two make up the big picture, four. Understanding comes with both sides of the brain working in harmony with the details and the big picture.

All areas of your life must be congruent with both sides of the brain working in mirror images to be healthy and efficient. Your brain also produces mirror—or double memories—in both hemispheres. Your brain was designed with both sides working in synergy, so the more you think, the more you understand.

There is so much more to this subject and I am only scratching the surface to help you understand the importance of healthy thinking. A great book for more in-depth information would be brain researcher Dr. Caroline Leaf's book, *Who Switched Off My Brain: Controlling Toxic Thoughts and Emotions,* published in 2009 by Thomas Nelson.

Where Did I Put My Keys?

Memory is a great and complicated thing. It serves us well and sometimes seems to get lost, often in moments of stress. But because of the double mirror memories, when calm returns, usually your memory returns as well.

Memory is stored long-term in the neuron cells. These cells are called dendrites and they grow, strengthen and pass information to other cells. They connect with other cells by way of synapses, electrochemically jumping from one cell to the other and creating more connections and feedback loops to your body. Your brain performs about four hundred billion actions each moment, and you are only conscious of about two thousand.

Spread your fingers out as you hold your arm up. This looks like a tree of sorts with your arm being the trunk called an axon and your fingers the dendrites or branches of memory. You have 100 trillion dendrites in your brain and each one can produce or grow 70,000 branches. This means you have about three million years of information capacity in your brain.

Your memory becomes strong by multi-sensory input and review of information within 24 hours, again in 7 days and ongoing. This strengthens the neuron cells by wrapping the axon trunks with myelin like a sheath to reinforce them. The brain cleans house at night and destroys cells that are not stable or strong. Have you ever lost information overnight and wondered why? Brain cleanup happened and your information was not reinforced enough.

The more senses you engage, the stronger your memory because your brain makes multi-sensory associations well. If you see, smell, taste and feel your burger, you will remember the experience of eating it better. You can strengthen the memory if you create an association with where you ate it, like imagining a large "Al" in your bun, or imagine you are sitting cross-legged on top of the Al's Burgers building eating this amazing burger with Al's sign flashing next to you.

When you have information that you want to remember, review it within 24 hours and again within 7 days and beyond and you will be amazed at how easy it is to remember long into the future.

Choose Your Attitude

There is more good news to all this information. You can choose how you think, thus affecting your health, well-being and positive successful behavior patterns.

You don't need a "happy pill" to change your brain chemistry; you need coping strategies.

This is how it works. The thoughts come in through your five senses: sight, hearing, taste, touch and smell. All but smell go to the inner brain limbic system, to the thalamus or relay station. Smell bypasses the thalamus and subsequent pathways and goes straight into the emotional storage center, the amygdala, which is why strong emotional memories occur with certain smells.

The electrical thought then gathers chemicals and goes on to the dendrites of memory where it looks for familiar information and memories. Dr. Leaf calls this a "breeze through the dendrite trees."

This breeze through the trees is your first attitude checkpoint.

This is your first chance to pay attention and decide to allow a thought to help or harm you. If the memory found in the cortex is negative or positive, the brain sends the emotional thought back to the thalamus and on to the hypothalamus, where it picks up more emotional chemicals.

You Can Control Your Thoughts

Now it gets dropped into the emotional library in the amygdala. The emotions stored here are strong and reactive. They can override any reasoning power you have, so your power of choice to analyze and choose healthy thinking is critical at this stage. This is your second chance to change your attitude and control your emotional thoughts.

You will always have a gut reaction from the emotions of the amygdala. Listen to your body so you can choose to analyze the thoughts that are creating those emotions. The amygdala has a direct link to the frontal cortex of reason so you can choose to put a love/faith spin on any thought, rewrite the emotional response and release the negative thought and emotion.

Consider if you were a student in class and a surprise math quiz confronts you. The thought, "I am not good at math," breezes through your cortex trees and lands on a memory of being told you are bad at math and a memory of a difficult experience with math in the past (first attention). Now the thought gathers more chemicals, drops into the amygdala and you have a gut reaction of stress and fear. Your stomach hurts, your heart pumps faster, etc. (second chance to take control). You have a choice to agree with the bad memory or choose a new thought like, "I am smart, I did my class work, I understand and I can do this," and literally rewrite the experience, emotions and reactions.

Turn Negative Thoughts to Hot Air

This is your third chance to change your attitude and control your emotional thoughts. The emotional thought now goes to the short-term memory, the hippocampus, and activates the "thinker" or corpus colosum, the C-shaped connective tissue that connects left and right brain responses. It allows you to access your reasoning skills at the front of the corpus colosum. With the benefit of the "thinker" in action, you *ask, answer and discuss* the whole situation with yourself, using both sides of your brain. You can now choose to allow the emotional thought to dissipate into hot air and not affect you negatively any longer. If you choose to hang on to the thought, it returns to the dendrites of memory and reinforces the negative or positive memory. The negative ones become black, thorny memory dendrites and continue to pump negative destructive chemicals to your body, while the positive ones become healthy, dense memories and promote healthy responses all over the brain and body.

Think back to math and ask yourself, "Is it true one hundred percent of the time that I am bad at math?" No. You are smart and you have done well at math at specific times. You now choose to have faith in your abilities, believe in yourself and know you can do math. Now it is easy to "thank your brain for sharing the negative," choose to ignore that negative and let it become hot air leaving your brain. Choose a true, good, positive thought instead. Choose to replace the negative emotional thought with a positive one. Then the negative thought cannot return to the cortex and become a long-term damaging memory.

Fear versus Faith/Love

> *"There is no fear in love, but perfect love drives out fear."*
> —1 John 4:18, New International Version Bible, 2009

All emotions stem from these two, faith/love and fear. Love- and faith-based thoughts are so much stronger than fear, even though fear can feel very strong when you are experiencing it. When you feel a sudden jolt of fear, the hypothalamus secretes a hormone called CRH dubbed the "negative emotion hormone" by doctors. CRH travels to the pituitary gland and stimulates another stress hormone called ACTH, which races down to the adrenal glands, releasing cortisol and adrenaline. This is not good news.

When these chemicals race unchecked through the body, they create adverse effects on your memory and cardiovascular system, causing high blood pressure, heart palpitations, aneurysms and strokes. They also attack the immune system, diminishing its effectiveness. You were designed for short bursts of stress, not an avalanche of stress or ongoing stress.

No wonder between 75 and 90 percent of visits to primary care physicians result from stress-related disorders, according to the American Institute of Stress.

For every negative thought and result, the converse is also true. When you experience faith and love and positive praise, recognition and support, you release good chemicals in the body, your cells and DNA are positively affected and you experience more wellness. Your memory is also stronger and healthier, and you become more intelligent. Your intelligence actually can continue to develop and grow as you age. It once was thought that you were born with all of your brain capacity and that it could not be changed. Now the research shows a great plasticity of the brain to grow and change for the good or bad. I encourage you toward the good!

Your Heart Has a Brain

Many neuroscience researchers now show that your heart actually has around 40,000 brain neurons that speak directly to your "free will" in the frontal cortex. Yes, science has discovered genetic free will.

"I want to know God's thoughts; the rest are all details."
—Albert Einstein, physicist and Nobel Prize recipient

It also has been proven that you are a spiritual being attached to a body and brain. When you are calm and thinking healthily, you can hear God or your higher power through your spirit and heart neurons talking to the brain. But if you are emotionally upset or thinking chaotically, you will not hear your heart at all. One way to know God's thoughts is to choose to be calm and listen to your spirit and heart.

Your heart brain is your last important chance to check your attitude. It is where you can tap into spirit and not only your good, but your *best* judgment.

Build Up Your Brain Power

The best news of all is that no matter what you have experienced, you can take control, stop and improve your brain function with the following steps.

1. Understand how thoughts and memory form.

2. Be alert and aware of your thoughts and the emotions expressed in your body. Never react to your first strong emotion. Stand back and analyze instead. Express your emotions calmly and healthily— no bottling them up. All emotions, positive or negative, become toxic when blocked.

3. Take every thought captive by using your intellect and attitude checkpoints. Protect what comes into your brain through your senses, especially what you see and hear.

4. Choose your thoughts. Positive "can do" thinking is healthy and feels great. Always replace negative excuses with positive faith- and love-based thoughts. Take responsibility and control.

5. Speak words out loud to frame your world because there are electromagnetic properties in your words, and the power to heal or harm you and others with them.

6. Use your thinker. Ask, answer and discuss everything with yourself. As you use both sides of your brain, be sure you are not making excuses or rationalizations for harmful thinking and behavior.

7. Accept uplifting emotional thoughts and reject negative ones.

8. Live in the NOW, or present. It is a gift, thus called the "present."

9. Contemplate "good" and meditate on words of positive, affirming truth. Soak in calm music and listen to your heart.

10. Be passionate. Passion is a healthy motivator and promoter of positive, healthy thinking. Dream on!

11. Be compassionate. Love and faith are the most powerful and healthy forces in the world. Think forgiveness. Love, hug, play and laugh a lot.

12. Exercise and drink half your weight in ounces of water daily, eat healthily, relax and sleep at least eight hours a night. Remember, your body feeds your brain and creates good brain chemistry. Take care of your body and brain.

My hope is that this chapter will whet your appetite and encourage you to take charge and learn more about your amazing mind, body and spirit connection. Remember, it is possible and important to think your way to health, happiness and success—all key ingredients in creating your incredible life.

CAROL STANLEY
That Special Touch

(253) 838-3511
carol@carolstanley.com
www.carolstanley.com

Carol Stanley is considered to be one of the most exciting trainers in North America, using the latest "accelerated learning" technologies and Biblical Truth. She is a dynamic seminar specialist and trainer who inspires and empowers people to phenomenal personal growth, physically, mentally and spiritually.

She is a graduate of CLASS (Christian Leaders, Authors & Speakers Services), Speak Up With Confidence, Peak Potentials' Experiential Learning Courses, and Toastmasters. Carol is a Certified Personality Trainer and is co-branded with CRG (Consulting Resource Group). She is the author of *Your Transformed Voice, Relationship Mastery, Beauty Is An Inside Job, Professional Image Mastery, and Life of Purpose* courses.

Carol is also a popular recording artist and radio and TV personality. She has spent 40 years as a professional fashion model, concert artist, voice teacher, actress, music and stage director, and presentation and life coach. Over that time, she has intensively trained in Bible principles, brain research, personality, voice and performance, as well as wellness and anti-aging technologies and methods.

She has shared the stage with legendary authors and trainers, including Florence Littauer, Zig Ziglar, T. Harv Eker, Debbie Reynolds and Jack Canfield, to name a few.

Connected Wellness
A New Paradigm for Health-Based Medicine
By Dr. Michelle Turcotte, ND

*H*ealth, hype and the media. You were made to enjoy perfect health and balance, but if you listen long enough to the media, you may buy into the marketing hype that your body has a drug deficiency.

The same force that created you also heals you. You are about to discover some life-changing truths that are not readily available to the public but that may save your life and start you on a journey toward better health and a more incredible life.

Rethinking cholesterol. Cholesterol is bad for you, right? Wrong, you need cholesterol; your body makes it anyway.

The following information is taken from *The Cholesterol Myths: Exposing the Fallacy that Saturated Fat and Cholesterol Cause Heart Disease,* by Uffe Ravnskov, MD, PhD, published in 2002 by New Trends Publishing, Inc. Many well-known scientists agree with Dr. Ravnskov, who can be found at www.ravnskov.nu/cholesterol.htm. His newest book is *Fat and Cholesterol are GOOD for you!,* published by GB Publishing in 2010.

A team of French researchers found that the death rate is five times higher for women with very low cholesterol. Increased risk of heart disease from cholesterol is present only in a small percentage of the population who have a rare inherited disease called familial hypercholesterolemia.

The famous Framingham project showed that almost half of subjects who had heart attacks had low cholesterol. In fact, the study showed that for each 1 mg/d. drop of cholesterol there was an 11 percent increase in coronary and total mortality. However, despite these clinical results, the American Heart Association and the National Heart, Lung and Blood Institute, in their review titled *The Cholesterol Facts,* stated: "the results of the Framingham study indicate that a one percent reduction ... of cholesterol corresponds to a two percent reduction in CHD (coronary heart disease) risk."

No one has been able to show that lowering cholesterol increases life span or makes you healthier. In fact, statin drugs can accelerate cardiovascular disease and stroke and possibly increase risk for certain cancers. Adverse side effects include liver damage, muscle damage and peripheral neuropathy. Statins are drugs used to reduce cholesterol. Statins also shut off your liver's ability to make HMG-CoA reductase, which is an enzyme used to make the antioxidant Coenzyme Q10. CoQ10 is needed by your heart and all cells to produce energy. This leads to congestive heart failure, which has doubled, coinciding with the use of statin drugs.

"If you are a woman, your odds of dying from breast cancer are 1 out of 27. Your odds of dying from cardiovascular disease are 1 out of 2. High levels of homocysteine, an inflammatory protein, can increase the chance of heart attack in men by 300 percent."

Statin drugs interfere with vitamins such as B12 and folate, resulting in elevated levels of a naturally occurring amino acid, homocysteine. Homocysteine is a leading marker for cardiovascular disease and leads to increased inflammation of the arteries that supply the heart muscle.

Plant sterols in raw fruits, vegetables and legumes lower cholesterol naturally. Always ramp down on drugs very slowly and supplement with CoQ10 while you find a healthy alternative. Good alternatives include alpha lipoic acid, polycosanol and formulations such as Cholest.

MYTH	FACT	HINT
High cholesterol causes coronary heart disease.	Cholesterol in the diet has only a marginal influence on the cholesterol in the blood. People eating less saturated fat and cholesterol actually tend to have higher cholesterol.	Oxidized cholesterol can cause plaque in arteries; do not scramble or fry your eggs. Low cholesterol increases risk for dying from cerebral hemorrhage by 500 percent compared to individuals with high cholesterol.
Vegetable oil is good for you; red meat and butter are bad.	Polyunsaturated fats increase inflammation & heart disease. Saturated fats can help stabilize cell membranes and improve immune function. Olive oil has omega-6 fatty acids; butter contains butyric acid and is a preventive for colon cancer. Coconut oil is great for energy and the immune system and is a health-promoting oil. Omega-3 fats in fish, flax and eggs feed your brain and immune system.	Polyunsaturated vegetable oils are found in almost all whole foods including meat, eggs, dairy, fruit, vegetables, grains and legumes. However, refined oils trigger oxidation and the formation of plaques. Never heat vegetable oils; cook with refined coconut oil only. Buy free-range animal products for high omega 3s.

MYTH	FACT	HINT
LDL cholesterol is bad and causes heart disease.	Only in one percent of the population with a metabolism dysfunction called Familial Hypercholesterolemia in which there is a lack of LDL receptors.	Increased heart attacks were the result of stress, overweight, lack of exercise and smoking.
Cholesterol blocks arteries.	There is no correlation between cholesterol levels and atherosclerosis. The Mayo Clinic found coronary atherosclerosis is increased in patients whose cholesterol had decreased by more than 60 mg/dl.	Cholesterol below 200 mg can increase chance of stroke. True risks for heart disease include obesity, diabetes and high blood pressure.
Unsaturated fats are good and saturated fats are bad for you.	Trans-saturated fats are bad because they cause disturbances in cellular function.	Saturated fats in limited amounts can help stabilize cell membranes and are building blocks for many hormones.
High-fat foods raise cholesterol	Studies find no statistical correlation between animal fat intake and cholesterol.	Cholesterol is controlled by factors other than diet. Stress can increase cholesterol rapidly by 10–15 percent.

Don't Be Fooled By Diet and Weight Loss Myths

Maintaining a healthy body weight is the key to living an incredible life. According to the Center for Disease Control and Prevention, obesity in adults has increased by sixty percent within the past twenty years, and obesity in children has tripled in the past thirty years. Thirty-three percent of American adults are obese and obesity-related deaths have climbed to more than 300,000 a year. Obesity is a major risk factor for cardiovascular disease, certain types of cancer, and Type 2 diabetes.

Obesity is defined as a body mass index or BMI of 30 or greater and is calculated by dividing your weight in pounds by the square of your height in inches. Finally, multiple this result by 703.

Let's go directly to a review of the contributing factors in weight gain and obesity taken from the outstanding research of Dr. Ann de Wees Allen, ND, Chief of Biomedical Research, Glycemic Research Institute in Washington, D.C. The following information can be found in Dr. Allen's *The Complete Guide to Fat-Storing Carbohydrates,* published in 2001 by the Glycemic Research Institute.

Certain carbohydrates stimulate fat storage while others do not because of their specific effect on insulin. According to Dr. Shari Lieberman's *Glycemic Index Food Guide,* published by Square One Publishers in 2006, the key is the glycemic index, or GI, a ranking system of the ability of a carbohydrate to elevate blood glucose and/or insulin. The ranking will determine if fat is stored from your food intake.

Glycemic load, or GL, takes into account the serving size, which determines the true glucose levels getting into the blood. A number of 20 or more per food item is considered high; 10 or less is low. A daily total GL of 80 or less per day is regarded as low, while a GL of 120 or more is high.

Glycemic load can be calculated as glycemic index multiplied by the number of carbohydrate grams, divided by 100.

Each GL unit is equivalent to 1 gram of carbs from pure glucose.

Anyone who has been on a quick-weight-loss diet has experienced the weight gain "rebound." This is due to LPL or lipoprotein lipase, the gatekeeper for fat storage. LPL increases dramatically during dieting. High glycemic foods that elevate insulin increase LPL activity in fat tissue in seven days. *LPL fat storing mechanisms can be eliminated by avoiding high glycemic foods.*

Stress can cause obesity as well as other physical and mental problems due to the release of two hormones, adrenaline and glucocorticoids, from the adrenal glands. These hormones raise blood sugar, which is then stored as fat if not burned off. Stress also stimulates the desire to eat high glycemic foods in order to increase the brain's neurotransmitter serotonin. Normal serotonin allows you to stop eating when you feel full after 20–40 minutes. If serotonin is low, you will continue to gorge on high glycemic foods. GTF chromium (polynicotineate, not picolinate) and tryptophan can help, as can chocolate. A bowl of low-fat chocolate ice cream with a low glycemic index can help satisfy these cravings without the weight gain and insulin elevation.

MYTH	FACT	HINT
Avoiding carbs helps in weight loss.	Low glycemic carbs are not as easily stored as fat. Combine low GI carbs with higher GI carbs to keep the insulin response low.	Particle size counts. The shape of pasta allows for slower digestion leading to a lower glycemic response.
Diabetics should eat high protein, but this is a good weight loss diet as well.	Insulin levels will increase when too much protein is eaten at a meal. High protein diets also make fat cells ten times more efficient in storing fat. Most weight loss is water.	Studies show that the recommended ratios are: carbs = 55 percent protein = 15 percent fat = 30 percent

MYTH	FACT	HINT
Sugar and high glycemic foods alone increase insulin leading to weight gain.	Insulin is increased by many factors, including coffee, alcohol, high fat and high protein, especially high protein without carbs.	Adding protein will increase glycemic response. Fat will lower the glycemic response of a high glycemic carb.

Abnormal weight gain due to genetic programming can now be successfully addressed. Over 40 years ago, a European medical doctor by the name of Simeon discovered the use of HCG, human chorionic gonadotropin, for weight loss in men and women. This hormone has been used safely for years to release stored abnormal fat in humans. According to Dr. Simeon's manuscript *Pounds & Inches, a New Approach to Obesity,* obesity in all its many forms is due to an abnormal functioning of some part of the body. *Persons suffering from this particular disorder will get fat regardless of how they eat.*

Dr. Simeon's HCG Diet is completely effective and safe when properly administered under the care of a licensed physician and has helped many people restore normal physiology and achieve healthy weight loss. *Many of my clients have lost a pound a day* on this program, restored normal blood sugar levels and kept the weight off. Studies reveal HCG may prevent and reduce breast cancer. Find a licensed physician that will screen you for sugar dysregulation, inflammatory markers, food sensitivities, liver/digestive function, hormone/neurotransmitter balance and the benefits of the HCG hormone diet.

Increase Your Exercise Awareness

Staying fit and active is a key factor in being healthy and enjoying a good quality of life. While you know the value of exercise, you may not be aware that conventional cardio workouts lose effectiveness after time and require increasingly more activity to achieve the same results. You need both aerobic and anaerobic exercise, but quality is more important than quantity and you should not overdo exercise in general.

According to www.howtobefit.com, certain fitness myths include:

MYTH	FACT	HINT
A lot of cardio is the most efficient way to lose body fat.	Excessive cardio will strip muscle and body fat. For each pound of muscle, you will burn up to 50 calories per day and muscle stimulates metabolism.	The proper amount of cardio is what is necessary. The AHA recommends moderate cardio 30 minutes a day, five days a week or vigorous cardio 20 minutes a day, three days a week.
There is one perfect workout routine.	The body will adapt to any routine in four to six weeks. Vary your routine every three to four weeks.	According to Stephen Holt, 2003 ACE Personal Trainer of the Year, limit your workout intervals to a max of 15 seconds to prevent lactic acid from blocking fat burning. Include a minimum of 22 seconds rest to reload myoglobin with oxygen.
Muscle weighs more than fat.	The difference is total volume; one pound of muscle is about the size of a baseball and one pound of fat is 3 times larger and looks like JELL-O.®	Check out FitVibe vibration exercise to reduce your hour of weight training to 20 minutes and balance your hormones.

Get Your Dazzle Back

Here are three steps you can take to bring you improved health:

1. Prevent disease with vitamin D3. More than 50 percent of the population is deficient in vitamin D. A team of research doctors at the University of California is participating in a study that they claim could save 25–50 percent of our national health care budget by restoring adequate vitamin D serum levels. According to Dr. Garland at Grassroots Health, (see www.grassrootshealth.net) the goal is to achieve levels of 40-60 ng/ml of D3 (not D2). Vitamin D3 at these levels prevents flu and colds; reduces risk and improves outcomes of over 16 cancers, including breast cancer; prevents diabetes, autoimmune disease, falls in the elderly and even reduces hypertension and heart disease. Go to www.joinDaction.org to participate in a study that can revolutionize your health.

2. Restore longevity and health. Enzymes and ionic minerals are indeed the "fountain of life" and are essential for every bodily function. Our diets are severely enzyme deficient, leading to a buildup of toxicity, allergies, autoimmune disease and aging. In fact, we lose ten percent of our enzymes every decade of life. Enzymes can reverse conditions such as Chronic Fatigue Syndrome, MD, Hashimoto's Disease and Benign Prostatic Hypertrophy (BPH), to name a few. Not all enzymes are created equal.

3. Regain your edge. You can achieve total health and longevity by balancing your brain. Dr. Eric Braverman, MD has pioneered an approach to balancing brain chemistry and preventing brain aging, which can reverse or prevent Alzheimer's, aging, memory loss, weight gain, sexual dysfunction and more. For example, low serotonin—discussed in diet and weight loss—also plays a role in other common disorders such as depression, seasonal syndrome disorders and PMS, in addition to obesity. Learn more about Dr. Braverman's revolutionary approach to aging and disease in *The Edge Effect,* published by Sterling Publishing Co. in 2005. In my practice, I have seen clients get off antidepressants, heart medications and regain youthful physiology by applying this medicine.

Health Care Reform

Make a good start on your own health care reform by implementing the information presented above.

- Make the decision to start now by writing down your health care goals.

- Verbally speak the goals out loud daily.

- Allow your subconscious mind to deliver the means to achieve your goals.

Doctor T's R$_x$ for Achieving Your Incredible Life

1. Stop eating foods with refined sugars of any kind.
2. Get your vitamin D3 levels up to at least 40-60 ng/ml.
3. Eat a diet of 55 percent low-glycemic carbs, 15 percent protein, and 30 percent good fats.
4. Exercise 150 minutes per week.
5. Take as few pharmaceutical drugs as possible.

Above all else: Stay positively connected to others.

With attention to my suggestions you will experience more balance, joy and of course, good health. All this will surely give you a more incredible life!

DR. MICHELLE TURCOTTE, ND
Avikai Connected Wellness

(888) RX-LOSE-FAT
(425) 450-0100
info@avikai.com
www.avikai.com

Dr. Turcotte is a naturopathic physician and a graduate of Bastyr University. She is also a founding member of the International Medical Spa Association, a member of the Washington Association of Naturopathic Physicians and the International SPA Association. Having graduated *cum laude* from the University of Washington in pre-med and psychology, her specialties include healthy weight loss and restoring balance through functional medicine. This knowledge has allowed her tremendous results with patients suffering from hormone imbalance, weight gain and mood disorders as well as epidemic diseases like diabetes, heart disease and cancer.

Dr. Turcotte's clinical research in combining western and eastern medicine has put her on the cutting edge of health-based medicine. Using medical counseling, Dr. Turcotte deconstructs health histories in order to rebuild a new and healthy future that she coins, *Journey of Renewal.*™ Her contributions to radio shows like Carol Stanley on the I'm Thankful Network have put her on the radar to becoming the next Dr. Oz of Natural Medicine. Look for Dr. Turcotte's new book, *Connected Wellness,* coming soon!

Your Elixir for Good Health

Find a Fitness Regime That Invigorates Your Spirit and Your Body

By Cori Ann Lentz, NASM CPT, ACE CPT, AFAA CPT

"Take care of your body with steadfast fidelity.
The soul must see through these eyes alone,
and if they are dim, the whole world is clouded."
—Johann Wolfgang von Goethe,
German poet, novelist, playwright and natural philosopher

*F*inding a form of exercise you truly love may be the magic elixir to realizing the true desires within your life. Research has shown exercise enhances your self-esteem, improves your mood, boosts your energy level, enhances sexual arousal in women, reduces erectile dysfunction in men, promotes better sleep and improves memory. If exercise is an elixir of health that enhances each of these areas within your own life, intoxicate yourself with pleasure.

"Movement is a medicine for creating change in a person's
physical, emotional, and mental states."
—Carol Welch, creator of Biosomatic Education

The first step to creating momentum toward health and harmony in your life is to achieve clarity of your true desires. Many of us have deeply rooted desires to be self-confident, strong, beautiful, energetic, sexual, healthy and to experience an overall higher quality of life.

Realize the Power of Fitness Within Your Life

As you contemplate your own personal fitness, pay particular attention to your thoughts, feelings and reactions. Many of us feel we have neglected our bodies and feel some form of shame, possibly expressing those feelings by becoming self-protective or defensive. If you notice this in yourself, please understand the human body is never meant to be shameful. Fitness is never meant to be punishment for enjoying a decadent meal or the tempting allure of your favorite treats. Motivating yourself with guilt over a piece of cheesecake or an extra glass of wine and punishing yourself with exercise is only going to create your inevitable rebellion instead of allowing you to embrace fitness as an attribute that enhances your life.

The information here is designed to inspire you to make a deliberate decision to have true respect for your body, no matter what state it is currently in. It is empowering to express yourself through your body, using movement to develop a sharp mind, attract success, achieve powerful personal development and discover a focused, purposeful life. The mind set you embrace while reading this and also while actually performing your physical activity is wholly relevant to this process.

The first key to your long-term, successful relationship with fitness is to find an activity for which you have true passion. It is important to find a physical activity with which you fall in love, looking forward to it each day and daydreaming about it just as much as you would a new lover. Building a respectful relationship with your own body, developing a true passion for moving your body and expressing yourself through your body are essential steps for fitness to become a realistic, long-term and healthy part of your lifestyle.

Expressing yourself through movement opens the door to physical, mental and spiritual growth. Physical fitness elevates your health, encourages dynamic and creative thought, promotes a state of mental well-being and can facilitate a breakthrough moment that is truly life-transforming. Physical activity is a wonderful opportunity to nourish and satisfy the cravings of your body, mind and soul.

> *"I always loved running...it was something you could do by yourself, and under your own power. You could go in any direction, fast or slow as you wanted, fighting the wind if you felt like it, seeking out new sights just on the strength of your feet and the courage of your lungs."*
> —Jesse Owens, American track and field athlete,
> Olympic gold medal winner

Playing-Out Instead of Working-Out

As children, we looked forward to running on the playground, jumping rope, playing foursquare, tag, kickball or anything to escape the tedious tasks performed at our desks. Revive that excitement as an adult through unique and inspiring forms of exercise that strengthen your body and also keep you motivated by entertaining you. Entertainment and fun are the most successful prime motivators for long-term behavioral change.

Innovative health clubs understand the importance of creating environments that are welcoming as well as entertaining. More important than that, though, is your own mind set. Protect yourself from the mind set of "furrowed-brow fitness," believing that fitness is a chore that must be done with a serious face, a specific number of repetitions, and a monotonous routine.

Many enjoy running because it is a time when you can effectively visualize your goals and start to make things happen with each step. Just as within your own life, you can choose to move at a gentle or quickened pace. You choose the amount of effort, time and sweat to invest and see the results your efforts yield.

"Wholesome exercise in the free air, under the wide sky,
is the best medicine for body and spirit."
—Sarah Louise Arnold, American author,
educator and founder of Girl Scouting

Any form of exercise you do outside can be an adventure and a chance to explore not only your surroundings, but also yourself. Research has shown that exercising significantly improves the higher mental processes of memory and executive functions of the brain that involve planning, organization and the ability to mentally juggle different intellectual tasks at the same time. While exercising, there are times when ideas flow naturally and even quickly to you with each breath. You feel energized and invigorated, which allows your creativity to surge. You may come up with new solutions to problems, new ways to do business or to communicate, or see things from a different perspective, allowing you to be innovative and enlightened.

Discover a Form of Exercise that Motivates You

Running, swimming, biking or any activity you do outdoors requires you to be flexible and adaptable to the world surrounding you. Hiking uphill can be a way for you to express how you take on life challenges as they come, taking time to appreciate the view, but also powering through the adventures. Take the lead and guide yourself to the top of your own personal mountain, just as you guide yourself to the top of your own personal accomplishments.

"I really don't think I need buns of steel. I'd be happy
with buns of cinnamon."
—Ellen DeGeneres, American comedienne,
television hostess and actress

Personally, I must confess that I detest running. There was a time that I was completely devoted to my early morning runs. I thrived on the adrenaline rush that came with them, even to the point of becoming a triathlete and a marathon runner. As my life changed, so did my preferences. Now, when I run I feel like a hamster on a wheel. I think of all the things I "should" be doing instead to build my business or care for my family. I count the minutes and the seconds, watch TV, read a magazine or blast my music to get through it. If I am forced to run on a treadmill, I may do all of those at the same time just to distract myself. This is the main reason I now engage in other activities instead of running. If you find yourself using the same "distraction techniques" when you exercise, understand it completely disengages your mind from your body and it may even diminish the mental benefits of exercise.

Fitness really is like intimacy within a long-term relationship: sometimes you have to mix things up to keep it interesting and exciting. Each time you engage in physical activity, it should be a rewarding, motivating and healthy experience. If you find yourself dreading exercise, distracting yourself to get through it or making excuses, try a different activity that you truly enjoy, like dancing, hiking, playing tag with the kids, hula hooping or a group activity where you feel exciting energy in a refreshing atmosphere, making it entertaining and enjoyable as well as healthy.

> *"Life is like riding a bicycle.*
> *To keep your balance you must keep moving."*
> —Albert Einstein, physicist and Nobel Prize recipient

Inspire Yourself with New Forms of Movement

I personally converted from "furrowed-brow fitness" to fabulously fun fitness. I enjoy and recommend hula hooping, Urban Strip

Tease™ Aerobics, dancing, hiking, jumping rope, barre fitness classes, boot camps and other unique forms of exercise that keep your mind and body wholly engaged in the activity, in addition to making you smile and laugh at yourself. While this list is hardly complete, my hope is that it inspires you to seek out activities that enhance your active and healthy lifestyle, in addition to informing you of new exercise concepts gaining popularity. There are several alternatives to better-known sports and exercise regimes. As always, it is recommended to consult your physician before you begin any exercise program.

Fun and unorthodox. Just say the words "hula hoop" and you cannot help but smile. Although it is unconventional, hula hooping is one of the only cardiovascular activities that primarily targets your core, giving you both cardio and strength conditioning. With circular trunk movements, it directly works abdominal muscles. Eight minutes of hula hooping burns as many calories as running an eight-minute mile, according to the Cooper Institute, a health-based, nonprofit research and education center. On average, hula hooping burns approximately 100 calories every 10 minutes. Hula hooping also promotes spinal and pelvic mobility in addition to correct body alignment.

Dance-inspired. Fitness programs inspired by dance or ballet barre work combine functional sport training with grace and poise, giving you a feeling of refined beauty. The Sports Barre,® The Bar Method,™ and The Dailey Method® each embody this philosophy within their fitness programs. Holding proper alignment and posture while focusing on abdominal strength, spinal flexibility and developing long, lean muscles keeps your mind engaged. This trains the entire body and mind while emphasizing effective body mechanics and creates graceful athleticism. Being completely focused and captivated by your own movements also strengthens the mind-body connection.

Alluring and provocative. One of my personal favorite new aerobic programs is exciting and taboo, which is part of the attraction. Bad Kitty Sassy Fitness,™ Flirty Girl Fitness™ and Urban Striptease™ Aerobics each combine the basic moves of a striptease with aerobic and body sculpting elements to create a fun, edgy and sexy workout. Your heart and body are pumping, melting the calories off, although your clothes actually stay on. These programs were created as a way for women to exercise, have fun and feel sexy in a safe, comfortable environment without any judgment.

> *"The more intensely we feel about an idea or a goal, the more assuredly the idea, buried deep in our subconscious, will direct us along the path to its fulfillment."*
> —Earl Nightingale, American motivational speaker and author

Transform Fitness to Enhance Each Stage in Your Life

It is important to recognize that your own preferences and abilities will change throughout different stages of your life. Learn to embrace and maximize those changes. During particularly stressful times in our lives, we tend to increase our activity level. Increasing physical activity as a way to cope with loss or stress is an effective and healthy way to improve your mood. Physical activity stimulates various brain chemicals that may leave you feeling happier and more relaxed.

It is important to find an activity for which you have true passion. This spills over into each area of your life, throughout each stage of your life. It provides your body with a relationship to your mind and allows for a lifetime of health and fitness.

> *"Learn to relax. Your body is precious, as it houses your mind and spirit. Inner peace begins with a relaxed body."*
> —Norman Vincent Peale, American author, professional speaker and minister

A woman can expect to live approximately one-third of her life in childbearing years, then one-third to one-half of her life past menopause. These are important changes within your body. No matter what stage of life you are currently in, it can be the most satisfying time of your life. Exercise plays a key role in making the transition through life-changing experiences easier, enhancing health, happiness and productivity.

The mood-elevating, tension-relieving effects of cardiovascular exercise help reduce the depression and anxiety that often accompany life-changing transitions. Cardiovascular exercise may also promote the loss of abdominal fat, a place most of us tend to store fat during stressful periods in life and during menopause.

Journal Activity

Introspection, truly understanding yourself, and giving recognition to your accomplishments are each important parts of making conscious, deliberate decisions. The ability to take control of your fitness directly correlates to your ability to take control of success within your own life. Keeping a journal is an easy way for you to facilitate this process. Reflect upon the seven areas listed below each time you begin a new exercise routine or make the decision to incorporate fitness into your lifestyle. Revisit the activity each month and expect the answers to change within each stage of your own personal development and growth.

1. Your body. What relationship do you currently have with your body? How have you felt mentally, physically and emotionally as your body has changed? Examples of changes would be childbirth, weight loss or gain, injuries or any significant changes within your life that have had an effect on your body.

2. The catalyst. At what moment did you decide to incorporate fitness into your life or to make this change? Please do a little introspection and be specific.

3. The lifestyle. What lifestyle changes have you, your family and your loved ones already adopted to work toward your goal? Examples would be scheduling childcare, nutrition changes or small changes to your daily activities, like taking walks with friends. How have these small changes affected you emotionally?

4. Secret weapon. What motivates you to exercise during times when you would rather not?

5. The challenge. What has been the hardest part of adopting fitness into your lifestyle? What pressures have you overcome? What family, work, childcare or other obstacles have you experienced?

6. Accomplishments. Above all, what do you feel proud of accomplishing this month? This does not need to be fitness related.

7. The fun. What part of this process have you found to be the most pleasurable?

Taking the time to have an in-depth moment of reflection for yourself not only shows respect for your body and your mind, but also commits you to the importance of your own health. This results in feeling admiration of not only your body, but also of yourself, and leads directly to true self-acceptance because of your in-depth understanding of the dedication and self-appreciation it takes to make your healthy lifestyle possible.

Exercise enlightens the mind, toughens the body and brightens the spirit. A balanced program includes cardiovascular activity, strength training and flexibility. The overarching theme is to engage in activities about which you are passionate. Movements that allow you to feel provocative, fun, elegant and powerful are going to keep you motivated and engaged. Enjoyment, fun and bliss are the prime motivators for successful, long-term behavioral change. The body craves new, adventurous ways to move. Love and respect those cravings by finding a fitness program that provides you with a positive experience.

CORI ANN LENTZ,
NASM CPT, ACE CPT, AFAA CPT
San Ramon Valley Fitness

Outrageously unique fitness instruction
to inspire you to get fit, love your body,
and feel fabulous!

(925) 359-1395
cori@sanramonvalleyfitness.com
www.sanramonvalleyfitness.com

Cori Ann has over twelve years in the health industry as a fitness professional, manager, seminar presenter and coach. She possesses nationally accredited certifications from the National Academy of Sports Medicine, American Council on Exercise and the Aerobics and Fitness Association of America. She also has specialty certificates in Advanced Program Design, Human Movement, Exercise for Special Populations, Pilates and Performance Nutrition. She is the founder and CEO of San Ramon Valley Fitness and the creator of The Sports Barre,® a method of exercise that takes an athletic approach to barre fitness, and Bad Kitty Sassy Fitness,™ a dance-infused, high-energy fitness program.

During her career, she found passion for teaching group fitness in addition to competing in triathlons and marathons. She is an instructor for the Schwinn® Indoor Cycling Program and Urban Strip Tease™ Aerobics. She is a master instructor and presenter in the Bender Method™ of Training.

Cori Ann divides her time between running a successful business, instructing group exercise classes, and caring for her husband and family of three children—plus three dogs. She believes that learning to exercise properly provides the body with a relationship to the mind, allowing for a lifetime of health and fitness.

Grandma Was Right

Simple Steps to a Healthier, Slimmer and Happier You!

By Tammy Tribble

"If you keep eating like that you will be as big as the broad side of a barn."
—Vessie Lillian Tuttle, my great-grandmother

Grandma was right. If you make food-related choices that are unhealthy, you can expect it to impact your body in a negative way. However, if you make more healthy decisions than unhealthy ones, you can expect to look and feel healthier, slimmer and more energetic. It will also positively impact your life and how you feel about yourself. In fact, I am sure you know the benefits of eating right and exercising. You might even qualify as an armchair nutritionist or dietician, based on the knowledge you possess about fat, calories and exercise. I would even bet you could tell me the calorie count in a portion of your favorite dessert. With all this amazing knowledge we possess and have at our disposal about food, exercise and lifestyle choices, how is it so many of us are still struggling to lose weight? In this chapter, I will cover some reasons why you may not have achieved weight loss success yet and will provide some simple, easy-to-use and powerful tools that will not only get you on track, but keep you on track until success becomes a lifestyle and being healthy becomes a habit.

I have struggled with my weight my entire life; I have lost and gained back literally hundreds of pounds in my lifetime. I have read every book and magazine on how to lose weight. I have fasted, cleansed, eaten meat, not eaten meat, counted calories, weighed my food, gone to meetings, written in a journal, trained, run a marathon, gotten a black belt in karate, taken supplements, and so on and so on and still my struggle with weight continued—and I am not alone. You may have a similar story to tell.

Your relationship with your weight can change and get better, even to the place where you feel good about your weight. After conquering my own weight challenges, today I coach, train and help people like you who have the genuine desire to lose weight, but are disillusioned with diets and want real-life solutions with real answers. What do you do when food is not just food? How can you break habits that have been a part of you for a lifetime? How can you lose weight without feeling different from your friends and family? How can you start a program without any history of long-term success? How can you possibly do it again and how can you make it work this time? The answer to these questions is what we are going to discuss in this chapter.

When Food Is Not Just Food

Emotional blanket. Ever heard of "comfort food," or had a special meal for a memorable event, or had holiday cheer with seasonal favorites? The fact is, food is not just food; it is bursting with memories, triggers and feelings. It is packed with baggage and sometimes becomes a tool for coping with the stuff in your life.

Reward or celebration. Were you ever bribed with treats when you were a kid, or fed ice cream or chicken soup when you were sick? Everyone has at least one psychological connection to food and most have more, many more. Have you ever said, "I just accomplished _____ so I deserve to go out to eat," or said, "I have been so good, I deserve a _____," or even said "Well, this is a special occasion, so I am just going to have one _____." The point is that it is universally acceptable to use food for reward, celebration and special occasions, and it started for most of us when we were kids.

Escape or denial. Have you ever used food to stuff your feelings or tune out from responsibilities? Have you ever eaten when you were not hungry just to take your mind off something or someone? Candy commercials promote escaping with rich chocolate delights and they are right. It tastes good and provides temporary respite from the challenges we all face at some time or other in our lives.

Food tastes good—sometimes great—but when it is used for comfort, reward or escape, your emotions are the ones calling the shots and your head is not involved until the aftermath of your unhealthy eating. Next comes the "Should and Guilt Cycle," which, repeated enough times, usually leads to extra unwanted pounds.

The "Should and Guilt" Cycle

The "Should and Guilt" cycle keeps you from experiencing the success you deserve and keeps you locked into emotional eating.

It starts with setting a goal that is too big. Have you ever said, "I am going to lose ___ pounds by _____," or promised yourself you will never eat _____ again? When you make a declaration to lose weight or place a food on the forbidden list, you mean it! You are absolutely sure that this time you will succeed and, in preparation for the grand goal, you eat all the foods that will soon be off limits. This is why you gain weight during the holidays, because of that New Year's resolution. Your mind is telling you to eat now because it will be gone soon.

Next comes intimidation, anxiety and overwhelm. This is what happens when you set a goal that is too large when you realize that your goal of ___ pounds by _____ is unrealistic and impossible without extreme measures. Even with extreme measures and immediate results, this continues to add to the anxiety because you know instinctively that you will not stay on such an unnatural eating regimen for long.

Intimidation, anxiety and overwhelm are followed by procrastination and excuses. This is the mind's way of protecting itself from the mental defeat of not accomplishing the goal. If you have enough excuses in your toolbox and have procrastinated on taking the necessary steps toward your goal, then when you do not succeed you will know you did not do your best, it sets you up for trying again at a later date and allows you to feel optimistic next time.

"Should" and guilt. "Should" is a troublemaker and it is always followed by guilt. The too-large goal, followed by emotional drama, is always followed by this delightful dialog of "I should have _____," or "If only I had _____." Then comes the guilt of not doing the things you should have done and, once again, not accomplishing the goal.

Reaction. You have your own coping mechanism for the disappointment and self-deprecation that comes from the "Should and Guilt" cycle. You may become moody, overeat or eat unhealthy foods to escape feelings or to find comfort. You may get stressed, run away or refocus your energy into an unimportant task.

Darn it! I did it again. This is when you realize that you are not going to accomplish the too-large goal or have already missed the deadline and not lost the pounds. This is a sad time and usually includes making up for the foods you were not allowed to eat while trying for the too-large goal, and sometimes includes weight gain.

New resolve, back to step one: setting a goal that is too big. This is when you have had time to recover your mental stamina and are ready to accomplish what you didn't before. Due to lost time on the last try, the goal is usually too large and the whole process starts again. How many New Year's resolutions have you set? How many times have you said, "I will be at ___ pounds by swimsuit weather?"

If this all sounds too familiar and seems depressing, recognize that you can break the "Should and Guilt" cycle and your dependence on emotional eating forever with the "Productivity, Goal Accomplishing, Feel Good" cycle. You do have the ability to get to your ideal weight.

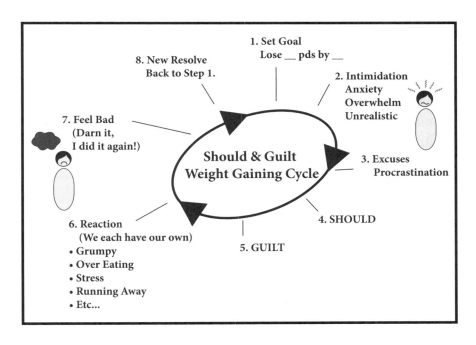

Special thanks to Neil Fiore, PhD author of *The Now Habit: A Strategic Program for Overcoming Procrastination* and *Enjoying Guilt-Free Play* [Penguin, 2007], www.NeilFiore.com

Break the Pattern of Emotional Eating:
The Productivity, Goal Accomplishing, Feel Good Cycle

This cycle keeps you empowered every day, builds upon your successes and keeps you motivated, while breaking a lifetime pattern of emotional eating.

It starts with a tiny, easy, manageable goal. The Half-Assed™ Weight Loss Plan breaks goal setting down into days, hours and minutes, into such easy and manageable steps that it takes away the fear of failure, because anyone can do that! Anyone can choose healthy for a day, or half-day, or even a half-hour! Once you accomplish the small, manageable goal, then it is easy to do the next, and the next, and the next . . . until healthy is a habit and you wake up thinner and happier than you were before!

Do one tiny thing toward the easy goal. If your goal is to make healthy decisions for one day, then for the next half-hour choose a healthy snack, meal or beverage. That tiny success builds momentum and catapults you toward the goal of one full day of healthy choices.

Feel good. Celebrate, pat yourself on the back and enjoy the feeling of the success. Feel in your body the positive feeling of taking care of yourself and making your goals a priority.

Keep taking tiny steps toward a manageable goal. Accomplishing small goals feels good and keeps you motivated and moving forward.

Feel better. This feels great! Success is becoming a lifestyle and the doubts and fears disappear as you continue to succeed.

Stay with the momentum. You know Newton's law that an object in motion stays in motion. That is what happens here, the stage is set for continued success, the small changes are adding up until success becomes a lifestyle.

Accomplish the tiny, easy, manageable goal. This feels fantastic! You feel empowered and liberated.

Set a new tiny, easy, manageable goal. Building on your history of success, you go into a new goal with the confidence that you can do it!

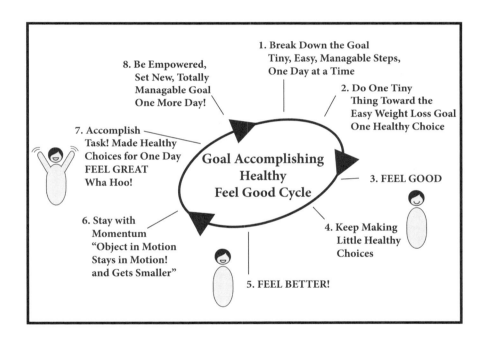

Special thanks to Neil Fiore, PhD, author of *The Now Habit: A Strategic Program for Overcoming Procrastination* and *Enjoying Guilt-Free Play* [Penguin, 2007], www.NeilFiore.com

Four Steps to Losing Weight while Eating the Foods You Love

How many times have you been on a diet and felt like you couldn't go out with friends? Have you ever gone to a party while dieting and felt different from the other guests? Have you ever turned down a delicious food because it was not on your diet?

The Half-Assed™ Weight Loss Plan encourages you to eat the foods you love while losing weight. It seems that as soon as you restrict a certain food, that food becomes your primary focus. By allowing the foods you love, they are no longer enchanting.

Here are four steps that work for weight loss success:

Step One: Be mindful! By adding awareness, you have the power to change the patterns and behaviors that have kept you overweight. I discovered so much when I kept a journal for a week. I figured out that I was having a glass or two of wine at five o'clock every day. This was my transition into evening and it had become a habit. Now I usually have hot tea, but occasionally, if I really want it, I have a glass of wine. I was waiting too long to eat, therefore I was getting overly hungry and moody. I started eating more often and found that I am satisfied with smaller portions and I feel more energetic. I am not suggesting you write forever, just long enough to figure out what patterns are standing in the way of your success.

> *"If you change the way you look at things,*
> *the things you look at change."*
> —Wayne Dyer, American author and lecturer

Step Two: Wait a half-hour. Anyone can "do" anything or "not do" anything for a half-hour. I started saying, "I will decide in a half-hour if I really want that (wine, chocolate, entire cake)." By stopping the momentum, it gives the brain time to be part of the process rather than just letting emotion or habit take over.

> *"From small beginnings come great things."*
> —Proverb

Step Three: Celebrate the success! If you chose to walk instead of driving as you usually do, then congratulations! If you chose tea instead of wine, then congratulations! If you still did the same behavior, but were able to add some mindfulness to it and delay it for a half-hour, then congratulations!

Always look for little things to celebrate that can make a huge difference, like drinking all the glasses of water you intended for the day, leaving a portion of food on your plate, getting up a little earlier so you can exercise a little longer. These are all things to celebrate.

> *"The more you praise and celebrate your life,*
> *the more there is in life to celebrate."*
> —Oprah Winfrey, American television icon

Step Four: Repeat steps 1–3 and do it again! And again, and again, and again, and watch your weight go down and your body confidence go up.

> *"Success is the sum of small efforts,*
> *repeated day in and day out"*
> —Robert Collier, American author

The Half-Assed™ Weight Loss Plan celebrates daily, half-daily, and even half-hour successes. The more times you succeed, the more times you will continue to succeed, and eventually you will find you have made healthy a habit and the old behaviors don't feel comfortable anymore. Imagine yourself thinner, more relaxed and happier than you have ever been before.

A friend asked me once, "How do you have a successful life?" The answer was having a series of successful days over and over. Same with the Half-Assed™ Weight Loss Plan. Small changes over time have big results. Even if you have never achieved weight loss success, you can have it now. Follow these simple steps, along with the "Productivity, Goal Accomplishing, Feel Good" cycle and begin living a life in which you know you are on the way to a healthier you.

TAMMY TRIBBLE
Doin' It Half-Assed™ Weight Loss Plan

Where success becomes a lifestyle and healthy a habit

(510) 881-8446
coach@half-assedweightloss.com
www.half-assedsite.com

Tammy Tribble is founder of the Half-Assed™ Weight Loss Program, an inspirational speaker, coach, mom and business owner. She credits her daughter as the inspiration for her weight loss program and is living testimony that small changes over time have big results.

She has committed herself to helping busy people everywhere learn to be healthier, more energetic and happier by applying her simple, fun and practical plan for nourishing the body and shedding unwanted pounds. She believes that success fosters success until it becomes a lifestyle and that healthy can become a habit. She believes that everyone has his or her own remarkable strengths and talents that can be channeled for weight loss success.

Originally from Texas, she lives in Northern California and still looks forward to going home to great Tex-Mex and Cajun cuisine. A graduate of California College of the Arts, she has a thriving graphic design business. She has a black belt in Kajukenbo Karate and loves teaching self defense. Having struggled with weight loss her entire life, she is confident in her own success and dedicated to helping others to live healthier lives, no matter what!

Leave Room for the Cream

Finding the Time to Enjoy the Richness
That Life Has to Offer

By Marilyn Ellis, CTACC

"How did it get so late so soon?
It's night before it's afternoon
My goodness how the time has flewn
How did it get so late so soon?"
—Dr. Seuss

While I was waiting in line at my favorite coffee house for my morning latte, the woman in front of me asked the clerk to "leave room for some cream." I thought, what a great title for an article on time management! Isn't that what we all strive to do: manage our time in such a way that we leave room for quality and richness in our lives?

Controlling our time is easier said than done. In the twenty-first century, we are all time jugglers, and it is only going to get worse as the information age and the technology age continue to overlap. Gone are the days of working for just eight hours a day and having the weekends off. Nowadays, jobs and businesses go far beyond an eight-hour day or a five-day workweek. With the advent of the Internet and cell phones, are we ever off duty? Employers and clients expect to be able to reach us anytime, anywhere. Even if we are in another time zone, surely we will check our email in the morning. It is also getting harder and harder to find time for family, kids' soccer games, vacations and friends, not to mention personal growth, personal health and community service, too.

What Is Time Management?

Is it really just as easy as trying to use your time wisely and getting all of your tasks completed on schedule? Well, yes and no. The most important thing to remember before embarking on any personal or business task is to realize that your time is the most precious thing you own.

Time, in fact, is the only natural resource that is totally non-renewable. You can't make it, find it when it's lost or take it back when it's spent. When time is gone, it is gone forever. As author Harold Taylor says in his book, *Making Time Work For You,* originally published in 1981 by Stoddart Publishing of Toronto, and Beaufort and Dell Pocket Books of New York, "Your time is your life."

Albert Einstein was fascinated with the idea of time travel. Indeed, his theory of relativity, $E=mc^2$ or energy equals matter times the speed of light squared, is a theory that can be applied to time travel. Einstein believed that time is not linear, but rather circular and if we could just move fast enough, we could bend time and return to where we started or somewhere in between. So far, it is only theory.

Time is the resource that we respect the least and waste the most. How many times have you heard someone say, "It didn't cost me anything, just my time." Learning to spend our time wisely takes some re-thinking and some courage. A few years ago, I had an opportunity to see and hear the famous physicist, Dr. Stephen Hawking, speak at the Paramount Theatre in Oakland, California. He was promoting his book, *A Brief History of Time.* Dr. Hawking, who uses a wheelchair, is the scientist who occupies the Newtonian Chair of Physics at Cambridge University. Even though he can now only speak by directing one eye to phrases listed on a voice-simulating computer, he is full of charm and wit. Dr. Hawking told the audience that one of his proudest moments was when he appeared in cartoon form on an episode of *The Simpsons.*

A member of the audience asked Dr. Hawking if he believed that time travel, as Albert Einstein envisioned it, would ever be possible. Dr. Hawking's reply was "No." Time travel would probably not be possible. Even if we were able to achieve time travel, our human form would surely not survive it.

If we are stuck with time as it now exists, what do we do when we have too many commitments and obligations and not enough time to accomplish them all? Well, if you think I am going to help you get more done in less time, you are wrong! What I am going to do is teach you how to work smart and right and not so hard and still accomplish what needs to be done.

Setting Your Priorities

Harold Taylor points out in his book, *Making Time Work For You,* that time is our most precious commodity. "Time management is not about getting more done in less time. Time management is about getting less things done but of more importance." Time is a simple organism. Did you know that there are only three kinds of time? Three is the symbol of completeness: three is the charm, three is a crowd, three strikes and you're out, The Three Wise Men, The Three Little Pigs, The Three Musketeers, three wishes. It is not surprising that time falls into this category, too. The three kinds of time are:

1. Things you must do and want to do

2. Things you must do but don't want to do

3. Things you don't have to do and don't want to do

Things You Must Do and Want to Do

This is time for yourself and those you love. This is your first and foremost priority—not job or other commitments. Schedule this time just as you would any other important thing that you must do and keep to it. If you have these things scheduled, you won't accidentally commit to something else and miss that anniversary dinner or child's soccer game or time with friends. You will exercise your body, your mind and/or spirit. These are the most important tasks that you have to do.

Quality of life is a respectable goal once more. What you have to do and want to do should include your job or business as well. If it doesn't include your job or business, then what are you waiting for? The mistake most people make is to try to cram their lives into nooks and crannies around their job or business. It should be the other way around. Creating a successful job and/or business around what you love to do and getting paid to do it is the greatest gift you can give to yourself. When you enjoy your work, it is time well spent.

Strive to engineer your job or business so that it compliments your life. That doesn't fit with the nineteenth-century work ethic in which we are still operating, does it? Welcome to the twenty-first century, where lifestyle really counts. When CNN medical expert Sanjay Gupta turned down the post of Surgeon General because it would take too much time away from his family, I knew the tide had finally turned. Quality of life is once again respectable. Go with the tide. Don't settle for less than a job or business that compliments your life. What can you do today to engineer your job or business to make that happen? What are you currently doing that is getting in the way of your personal life?

Things You Must Do but Don't Want to Do

You can't just drop everything and have fun! The world still needs to function. These activities might include mundane activities such as mowing the lawn or shopping or paying the bills. In business, they might be writing reports, filing or billing or inputting data, meetings and business trips.

Re-evaluate if they need to be done at all. Do not be afraid to challenge the status quo. Some things have been done for so long that their original purpose has been lost. Many reports are redundant. Is anybody reading them?

If it truly must be done, delegate the task to someone else. Hire someone if you have to. Pay someone to play at what you have to work at. Do what you love and delegate the rest. What can you delegate to others right now so you can stop doing the things you don't want to do?

Things You Don't Have to Do and Don't Want to Do

Here is where it gets really tricky. How do you define this category? Isn't everything you are doing important? Besides, you are not a quitter. You already promised to do it.

Most successful people suffer from "Gee, that sounds like fun" syndrome. Are you a pleaser, afraid to say "no" because someone might not like it? Do you think everything sounds like so much fun or is so worthwhile that you must be a part of it? Do you think you are the only person who can really do the job?

Here's a strategy for determining what you really don't have to do: Patient to doctor: "It hurts when I do this." Doctor to patient: "Then don't do that." If you don't like doing it anymore, then stop doing it. If you dread and postpone what must done, it falls into this category. If that includes going to your job or business, then you need a new job or business. If it is committees or councils or clubs that eat up your time without giving you any personal returns, get off those committees and councils and leave those clubs. It doesn't matter whether you already said "yes" or have been doing it for years and everyone depends on you. Stop doing it right now. I give you full permission not to feel guilty. Submit your notice right now and start focusing your life and time on the things that feed you spiritually or financially.

Learn how to say "no" or "goodbye" and still leave them smiling. It is easy to be caught off guard when asked to be on a committee or council. You like the person. You are honored to be asked. The cause is a good one. Here are some friendly but firm ways you can say "no" without offending anyone. Memorize these, write them down and post them by your telephone:

- "I just haven't got the time right now. It sounds like a wonderful program. Why don't you check with me again next year."

- "I know I said I would do it, but now I find that I don't have the time to give it the attention it deserves."

- "I know I have been (on this committee, coaching this team, head of this group) for a very long time. Now I feel it is time for me to step down and allow someone else to bring new energy and ideas into the group."

You are more important than your obligations. It's true. Committees and councils need volunteers. Your time and contributions have been valuable to them, but your time is more valuable to you! There will be other people to take your place as you move on to more important things. Let go of the outcome and grab on to opportunities to do what contributes to your well-being, your family and your cause. Let go, and live on!

No More Excuses—Put Yourself First

Making excuses that prevent you from taking action just makes matters worse. My favorite quote from Lewis Carroll's *Alice In Wonderland* is when Alice says, "The hurrier I go, the behinder I get." When we are "too busy" to fix a problem, all that happens is that we get older and the problem gets bigger. The resulting damage done to a neglected body, mind, friendship, relationship, marriage or business is that much harder to fix. We tell ourselves, "I haven't got the time to figure it out now. I'll do it later." Excuses for later are:

- I can't afford to hire someone.
- I'll get organized after I finish this project.
- I'll go to the next soccer game.
- I'll be able to take the family on that vacation next year.
- I can't leave now; they need me.
- I'll do it when the kids finish school.
- I'll do it when the kids go back to school.
- I'll do it when I get my new computer.
- I need to get my stuff organized before I hire someone to help.
- I'll do it in the spring/summer/fall/winter.
- If I don't do it myself, it won't get done.
- I'm the only person who can do it.

Get off your assets and just do it. If time is a non-renewable, precious resource that represents your life, then what are you waiting for?

- **Is it feeding you spiritually or financially?** Managing your time so that it includes only what feeds you spiritually or financially is using your time wisely. It is a great litmus test for what to keep in your life and what to discard.

- **What does "spiritual" mean in the context of time management?** Does the activity you are spending your time doing uplift you, transcend the mundane? Does it make you feel happy and satisfied? Does it inspire you, tap into your creativity, feed your family and love relationships? In other words, is it worth spending your precious life doing?

- **What does "financial" mean in the context of time management?** Consider your time a form of currency. How you spend it and with whom you spend it will determine your return on investment (ROI). It will tell you where your priorities are. Whether you have a job or own your own business, is it giving you a good ROI? Are your personal activities giving you a good ROI? Are the people you are giving your time to giving you a good ROI? It may seem selfish to consider yourself, but as we are told in airplane emergencies, put *your* mask on first!

- **You have a right to be happy.** Somewhere in time, many of us were taught to believe that we weren't meant to be happy in this life. The truth is that you deserve to live a happy, productive and interesting life right now. If you haven't got that now, when do you plan to have it?

Recognize the Business Vampires

How many times have you been asked to help someone on a task they could easily complete themselves? They are time vampires. Tell them you are certain they can do it themselves and wish them the best of luck. Screen your calls. Alexander Graham Bell never had a telephone in his home as he thought it was a terrible intrusion. You don't have to answer the phone just because it rings. Do you really need to take that business trip or could the meeting be held virtually? Teleconference meetings not only save time but money and energy as well. Go "green" whenever possible.

Recognize the Personal Vampires

Personal vampires are the people who are always in trouble and need your help. They could be colleagues, friends or the black sheep in the family. You listen to their problems and offer help and advice, which they never take. They really don't want your help—they want your time, energy and attention. Learn to cut them off quickly or eliminate them from your life altogether. Don't worry, they will find someone else to suck the time out of.

If you have a great idea, be careful whom you share it with—not because they might steal it, but because chances are they won't understand it and will give you a million reasons why it won't work. It will paralyze you, delay your getting started or slow you down considerably. Many great ideas have been killed by personal vampires.

Have no regrets. My senior clients tell me all the time that it is not what they did that they regret the most, but what they did not do. You only have one life, so live it completely.

Your time is the most precious thing you own. If you are not happy now, when do you plan to be happy? Treat your time as a treasure to be protected, shielded and cherished beyond anything else. If you do that, you will enjoy the richness that life has to offer—you will have left room for the cream.

MARILYN ELLIS, CTACC
Lighthouse Organizers, LLC

Helping people navigate through their busy and challenging lives

(925) 943-5571
mellis@ecis.com
www.lighthouseorganizers.com

Marilyn Ellis has a lot of people listening. As an author, speaker, certified coach and professional organizing dynamo, she not only helps people "get organized" but she also helps them "think organized!" Her company name, Lighthouse Organizers, LLC, reflects her true desire "to help people navigate through their busy and challenging lives." If you are stuck on the rocks, lost in the fog or surrounded by sharks, Marilyn will shine her harbor light on you and bring you home safely.

Marilyn is a third-generation San Franciscan and graduate of San Francisco State University. Her certified coach training was obtained at Coach Training Alliance in Boulder, Colorado.

She is a member of NAPO, MDBW, NASMM, and is past president of the SF East Bay Chapter of the International Coach Federation. She is the proud mother of two and lives in Walnut Creek, California, with her husband, Neil, and her beloved birds and border collie.

Marilyn is the author of *How To Succeed in Your First Year As An Entrepreneur* and *What Do You Want Your Business To Do For You?* She speaks extensively around the country on business and life topics.

The Bulletproof Woman
Dissolving the Shields Between You and Love
By Kimi Avary, MA

*I*n relationship coaching, I see many women who have shields protecting their hearts. We call her the Bulletproof Woman. She is strong, successful and social. She has a good job or owns her own business. She is passionate, confident and has goals. She learned that she could have it all, but she is strangely unfulfilled, exhausted, and at times feels lonely. She has learned how to survive in a man's world by putting on a bulletproof shield that has also kept her alone and isolated in her romantic personal life. She craves intimacy and doesn't know how to get it. She doesn't have the greatest boundaries: she either loses herself in relationships or shields herself in a way that keeps her from connecting with potential partners. She has often confused chemistry for love and has dived into one relationship after another only to find that she was not happy because she ignored red flags and deal breakers. If she is married, she might not have the depth of intimacy she craves.

The goal here is to give you illuminating tools that will start you on the road to having a more fulfilling relationship experience with your partner and with everyone with whom you come into contact. I will be sharing tools for relationships and ten integrated principles that have made it possible for thousands of women and men to have and keep the relationships they have always dreamed possible. This relationship model might be different than what you have heard before, and I invite you to look for the ways it may fit for you rather than how it doesn't.

You have probably heard of the story about the princess and the frog. She is supposed to kiss the frog, and he is supposed to turn into an incredibly handsome prince, and then they are to live "happily ever after." Well, quite often the reverse happens. You kiss a perfectly great man, and pretty soon he becomes a frog. What happened? No one walks down the aisle thinking that they are marrying a jerk. This experience can be long and drawn out or short, but either way, it is agonizing. A strong instinctual foundation drives the behavior differently for men and women. Let's explore those differences and get some hints on how to keep the prince.

Feminine and Masculine

One problem is that women see men through their eyes as women, and men see women through their eyes as men. Women expect men to do things the same way they do. Men, too, are frustrated when women don't do things the way they would. We each think the other person is wrong or misbehaving. With each frustration, our shield gets stronger and we feel more separated.

The sad truth is that we have been led to believe that we are all the same, and that we can do all the same things equally well. In reality, we are quite different biologically and for excellent reasons. It does not mean that we cannot learn how to do things that our mate can do—it means that we are wired differently, we have a different nature and it does not have anything to do with intelligence.

For example, think in terms of the gatherers and the hunters. The gatherers tend to be women and the hunters tend to be men. The gatherers have a diffuse awareness that pours into every direction, and the hunters are singly focused on hunting the deer. Gatherers scan the meadow and fill their basket with everything they see that is edible. It would not go so well if they focused on getting one item at a time. The hunters, on the other hand, would not be bringing home dinner if they were not focused and committed to getting that deer. They may get another deer, or rabbit or antelope too, but that will happen only when they have secured the first one.

We all have feminine and masculine energies within us. It's like Yin and Yang—two sides of the same coin. They balance each other and neither one is better. To be feminine is to be receptive, adaptable, eternal and flowing. To be masculine is to be proactive, productive, time-bound and committed. The more masculine one person is, the more feminine the person they draw to them will be. This is not about stereotypes of flowers and lace or machismo. This distinction is not dependent on gender; however, women tend to be more feminine and men tend to be more masculine. It will depend on the context whether the feminine or masculine energy shows up.

For instance, a woman who works in a masculine career that requires her to be single-focused, productive and strong might develop a shield that protects her in the business world. This shield that serves her well at work and makes her a great buddy with co-workers also prevents intimacy. You see, if a woman is in hunt mode and wants a relationship, she has a problem—hunters do not date other hunters. If a woman wants to be with a man romantically, she needs to let down her shield and transition into being feminine. One thing I recommend for doing this is to get into your body by taking a delicious-smelling, candle-lit bath, listening to sensual music and putting on lingerie that feels great against your skin, is comfortable and makes you feel amazing. Taking the time between work and a date to transition into being feminine will help you put your shield down. Even if the date has to start later, it will serve you because you will experience deeper intimacy and connection.

Next, we will be looking at ten principles for creating a great relationship. If you are already married, review these principles to see where there is room for you to upgrade the relationship you currently enjoy.

Principle #1: Know Who You Are and What You Want

Invest the time to discover who you are and what would make you happy. Seems obvious, right? A woman by nature is flexible and adaptable to those she cares about and to those around her. She tends to meet someone and lose herself in the relationship. She goes into adaptable "pleasing" mode. Being true to yourself is much easier when you are single, so before you are in a partnership, it is important to articulate with clarity who you are and what your life's purpose is. This will help you set a strong foundation for meeting and keeping the perfect partner for you.

Principle #2: Learn How to Get What You Want

Because of our adaptable nature and our tendency to support others, getting clarity about our wants and needs can be challenging. It often takes being supported by someone whom you trust so you can let your shield down and truly assess your situation. What tools do you need? What skills do you need to learn? What fears, limiting beliefs and attitudes hold you back? Did you know that you can consciously choose the attitudes that serve you and support your life goals, and let go of those that sabotage you? With support, you can develop strategies that feel good to you and create an action plan that leads you to your goals.

Principle #3: Be the "Chooser"

Being the *chooser* means taking initiative and responsibility for the outcomes in your life. Being a chooser is about knowing what you want and how to get it, and holding true to what is important to you.

Many singles have the belief that there are not enough single people to go around. There are over 101 million single adults in the United States alone—that's forty-six percent of the population. That means there is no scarcity of singles, but a scarcity mentality.

Often, we are afraid that what we want is unattainable, so we take whomever comes into our lives. As women, we tend to start relationships easily and end up in a relationship because it is there, not because it is the right one for us. We experience tremendous pain when we stay because we feel obligated and cannot bring ourselves to break it off, or we feel like we have failed at another relationship. By being the chooser, we drop our shields for love.

Principle #4: Balance Your Heart with Your Head

Our culture encourages us to look for someone with whom we have incredible chemistry. Just look at romantic comedies. They are about love at first sight, being swept off our feet and living happily ever after. When dating, our friends ask us if there is chemistry. Chemistry is great, but unfortunately, chemistry alone does not make a great relationship.

Of course, chemistry needs to be there, but you also need to balance it with your *requirements, needs, and wants* to make conscious relationship choices. Doing this will help you feel more comfortable and be clear in your interactions, as well as help you focus on potential partners and become really good at weeding out the rest. You will also feel more comfortable in dissolving your shields between you and love.

Principle #5: Be Ready and Available for Commitment

You may want a relationship or are already in one. Do you have a shield between you and love? Are you complete with past relationships?

Do you have financial, family or legal obligations that need some attention or clearing? Creating an amazing relationship takes being attentive to our lives and being conscious. If we are not, it puts unnecessary pressure on the relationship. You need a clear plan for creating a healthy foundation on which to build your relationship. It would be a tragedy to meet your soul mate and not be ready or available because you had not attended to your life. Get your life in order.

Principle #6: Use the Law of Attraction

Focus on creating the life you want and imagine your partner there with you. Visualize the two of you being together and doing the types of things you want to do as a couple. By putting your shield down, you have started on the path of creating space for a partner in your life. "Like attracts like." Therefore, express the traits that you want your partner to have. If you have a shield between you and intimacy, the partner you find will be shielded, too. Prepare your environment for your mate. If you have a two-car garage, park on one side instead of the middle. Do the same with your bed. Remember that if you focus on what you don't want, you will be drawing that to you, so focus on what you do want.

Principle #7: Gain Relationship Knowledge and Skills

Become a researcher, and have an open spirit for new ways of relating. Take the time to enhance your relationship skills. Learn how to deepen your relationships. Enjoy the dating experience as an opportunity to practice your skills. Read books. Hire a coach to help integrate what you are creating in your life. Open your heart. Take relationship classes and workshops. The key to successful relationships lies in uncovering what you don't know, because it is the gaps in your knowledge and your blind spots that cause relationship problems.

Principle #8: Create a Support Community

No matter where you stand, in "singleness" or "coupleness," you need a community of people outside your relationship to enhance your needs. People get into trouble when they expect one person to meet 100 percent of their needs. Singles looking for that one person are setting themselves up for failure, and couples who are isolated tend to break up. It is more realistic and appropriate for you to get about 25 percent of your needs met by your partner. Community friendships will help you gain and hone your skills, as a way of preparing for, finding and keeping a successful relationship. They will also bring you joy.

Principle #9: To Dissolve Your Shield, Learn Assertiveness

Being assertive requires setting boundaries, which is very different from putting up your shields. You must say "no" to what you don't want, and "yes" to what you do want. Most women with whom I work are challenged by this, and instead of having healthy boundaries, they are shielded. Saying "no" is a complete sentence. Being a pleaser and adapter often feels safer than stating our boundaries, and what will or will not work. Often we think we are being assertive, but it is actually demanding and usually comes with a tone that says, "If you don't do it my way, you will be punished." This attitude comes from assuming that he knows what you want and is deliberately not doing it. Over time, we make the judgment that he doesn't love us enough to do the right thing. Additionally, when a man is assertive about something he needs, from our viewpoint, he looks like a jerk. We would never want people to think of us as a jerk, so we adapt. Practicing assertiveness can be scary, but by not doing so when you can, you are actually choosing to live the life you are living, instead of the life you really want. The tendency is to blame the other person for your unhappiness. Unfortunately and fortunately, the only person responsible is you.

Principle #10: Be a Successful Individual

Successful individuals make great partners. By living your life purpose and vision, you will be happier. The happier you are, the better you will feel about yourself and the more attractive you will be. Ask yourself if you are happy and successful when you are on your own. Personal success makes relationship success and satisfaction a lot more likely.

You were not born with a manual on how to have incredible relationships, so take the time to get to know who you are and what you want. Take opportunities for self-exploration and learning. Take steps to dissolve your shields so that you can balance your heart and your head in choosing your partner. Know your requirements, needs and wants, and be assertive about them. Practice the law of attraction. Create a support community that brings you joy. Utilize a coach to help you focus, stay true to yourself and manifest the perfect partner and relationship for you. You deserve it. You can have it. It all starts with you.

KIMI AVARY, MA
The Bulletproof Woman

Dissolving the shields between you and love

(800) 462-1545
kimi@bulletproofwoman.com
www.bulletproofwoman.com

Kimi Avary has more than 15 years of experience successfully coaching clients to have winning relationships. Her clients are women and men who are relationship oriented, ready to meet and receive their life partner and deepen that partnership into a joyful relationship. She guides her clients from the inception of dating and into healthy relating by utilizing a multitude of tools, including one-on-one coaching by phone and a five-stage, state-of-the-art curriculum. She specializes in dissolving the shields between you and love, helping you to clarify your relationship goals, leveraging the law of attraction principles, communicating effectively with the opposite sex, and creating fulfilling relationships. She works with individuals and couples in creating relationships that are both functional and satisfying.

The foundation of love, connection, joy, vibrancy and integrity enlivens her work with clients. She holds the premise that men and women are different, well-made, and want to give and receive love. She is an intuitive, insightful coach, passionate workshop leader and professional speaker. She holds a Masters in Counseling Psychology, is a Relationship Coaching Institute Certified Coach, is an NLP Health Certified Master Practitioner (Neuro-Linguistic Programming), and a Pax Programs Licenced Partner. Pax Programs is the creator of the Celebrating Men, Satisfying Women workshop series.

Prosperity and Good Fortune
Creating an Incredible Financial Life
By Debbie Whitlock

*T*he roles we take on as women are many and varied. In some ways we are like balloons with the ability to expand to our maximum capacity. Yet, just like the balloon—with too much, we will pop!

Are you the CEO of your home, the executive of the family? You may have the color-coded calendar representing each child and each activity—you are probably the family driver—you coordinate *your* social calendar, your *child's* social calendar, and you volunteer. You make sure the house is kept up and while you are so busy "keeping up," over time you may have made some decisions to not be involved with the things that you just don't have the time or perhaps the interest in "keeping up" on—the long-term financial strategy for you and your family.

You are the accounts payable department in your life, you have negotiated the best deal on your Internet and home phone provider, you have an awesome deal on your family's cell phone plan, and you know to the dime where to get the best deals to stretch your family's grocery budget—but you are not the CFO in your life. Along the way, "retirement" and the long-term financial goals you had set for yourself took up a position in the "optional third-row seat" of life. It has become the thing you will get to later.

I invite you to move your financial knowledge and engagement to the front seat and begin transitioning to CFO of your life.

Because, what if life happens? A moment of crisis will not be the best time to pay attention to your financial situation.

I am certainly not suggesting that you will be prepared for all financial possibilities headed your way if you follow the tips I am about to share. However, I do believe you can be better prepared, so that when the day comes to move forward, you can have a strategy in place.

Remember, knowledge is power and knowing is better than not knowing, and once you *know what you don't know*—you can begin to create a personal path to get you from where you are to where you want to be. I invite you today to take what may be for some of you the first step on the journey to becoming the CFO of your life. For those of you who are there—congratulations—re-commit, re-examine and re-define your financial situation, your financial knowledge and your financial literacy.

Our financial independence as women is much better than it was just fifty years ago, and there is definitely good news for us women and our finances: according to a FiLife Study in conjunction with the *Wall Street Journal,* women are better at investing than men, and are more likely to participate in a retirement plan, and in the 2009 report, *A Woman's Nation Changes Everything,* we learned four out of ten mothers are the primary breadwinners, bringing home the majority of the family income.

And still with all this good news—we as women have a long way to go.

According to www.soundinvesting.org, in 2009, 40 percent of married women were still not involved in the decision-making process of the family finances; women wait two to four years longer to start saving for retirement; and in recent reports it is estimated that one in ten female retirees and one in five single women over the age of 65 live on less than $10,000 per year!

The Wake-Up Call

In general, women:

- Earn less
- Live longer
- Spend less time in the workforce
- Must address the "what-ifs" of life

Women Earning

On average, women still earn less than men according to the Institute for Women's Policy Research. While the wage gap has been closing over the past twenty years, it is still there. This disparity in earning puts women at a distinct disadvantage when planning for retirement. Lower earnings mean less money to contribute to retirement plans, which will result in less money for income in retirement.

In a June 2008 article published by the Department for Professional Employees entitled "Professional Women: Vital Statistics," they found on average, families of working women lost out on $9,575 per year because of the earnings gap. Over time, this adds up to a very significant loss. In the twenty years between 1984 and 2004, women had lost over $440 million in earnings because of the gender wage gap.

Women Living

Statistically, women live longer than men. According to the U.S. Census Bureau, in January of 2009, at age 85 and over, there are *twice* as many women as men.

This means if you are married, you have a good chance of outliving your husband. In January of 2009, www.soundinvesting.org found: 71 percent of the elderly are women—of this group, 48 percent are widowed and 80 percent of the widows now living in poverty were not poor before their husbands died.

Between 1950 and 2005, the number of women age 65 and over more than tripled, increasing from 6.5 million to 21 million. Additionally, the U.S. Census Bureau projects that by 2030, the number of women aged 65 years and over will double to 40 million.

The chances are good whether you are a single or married woman, you will live a good *long* time in retirement. Will what you have saved support you throughout your many years of retirement?

By earning less and living longer, a woman's assets must work harder for a longer period of time.

Women Working

Here's the third piece—as women we typically leave the workforce more often than men. Why? First, to have children, then to care for children and, a phenomenon occurring more and more frequently, to care for our aging parents. These are all very important and necessary responsibilities, coming at a significant financial cost.

Uncontrollable Variables—The "What Ifs" of Life

To a certain degree, we can control how much money we save, but we can't control inflation, the stock market or, to some extent, how long we will live. Unexpected life events can and will occur.

For married women—you are probably planning your savings and your retirement based on two incomes. What if you get divorced or your husband dies? Chances are good your income will be drastically reduced—perhaps up to 50 percent and possibly more—but guess what—one does not necessarily live significantly cheaper than two and your total expenses are typically reduced by fractions in comparison to the loss of income you would experience.

Are you prepared to make up the possibility of a significant shortfall?

What to Do

Where do you start? Like any big undertaking, it is best to break it down into realistic stages.

First—Identify and prioritize your goals. What are you saving for? Remember, your goals must be specific. Write them down.

Are you saving for a down payment on a home? Paying for your child's college education? Opening or expanding your own business? Purchasing a second home?

How much will you need? What is the time frame? Is it attainable?

The next step is to prioritize these goals. Think about where you are in life. What goals need to be accomplished soonest? What goals will take the longest to reach? Give yourself the opportunity for "small wins" along the way—it gives you tremendous confidence and validates you are on the correct path.

Now that you have gotten clear on your goals, don't just tuck them away in a drawer or a file, keep them out where you can see them every day. Post them on the mirror where you get ready in the morning, or near you in your office—seeing your financial goals every day will keep you on task. Even keep them in your wallet or purse. Reviewing your goals and making them a priority will help you make good choices with your money as you go through your life.

Once you have your goals and priorities in hand, what do you do next?

Second—Develop a budget and a plan. Understand a budget does not have to be a system of punishment—and a constant reminder of what you cannot have. It really does help you understand how money flows into and out of your life.

When you are developing a budget/spending plan, start by examining your spending habits.

One way to start is to write down every purchase—yes, every cup of coffee and snack, every lunch and impulse item. All of it—for a set period of time.

Take a good hard look at where your money is going. Look for opportunities to eliminate unnecessary spending. What is that latte a day really costing you? Is it keeping you from paying down credit card debt? Contributing to an emergency bucket of money for yourself? Contributing more to your retirement account? You may be thinking, "But it's only $3.50/day, that won't make a difference." It will. That $3.50 coffee per day is more than $1,200 per year. That is the cost of a vacation! Would you be willing to have coffee at home—and take an extra trip this year with cash? What about lunch out? Too busy to put a sandwich in a bag before you head out the door and instead dash into your local sandwich shop to grab a quick midday bite? Say the average cost of lunch out is about $9—you do that five days per week multiplied by 52 weeks per year, and you will be spending more than $2,300 per year on lunch out.

It is important to not dismiss the expenses in your life that don't seem significant; it really all adds up.

If you are willing to give up the coffee and the lunch in exchange for a great vacation or acquiring money toward something you *really* want—the money will not magically remain in your life unless you consciously move it. Each lunch you don't eat out will have you making a $9 contribution to a separate account, specifically to hold the money you are saving, now that you have committed to being a conscious consumer. It won't be enough to just "not spend"—you want to be able to visually see the reward of saving.

The next step is to avoid high-interest debt—like credit card debt—or pay it off if you have already incurred it. Those high interest rates will eat away your savings, making it extremely difficult to achieve your financial security. The finance charges associated with credit cards will have you constantly feeling as though you are taking one step forward and two steps back, when you are making minimum payments and continue spending on credit. Credit cards are a very twentieth century phenomenon—it was not until the magnetic strip was established as a standard on the back of your card in 1970 that credit cards really became a significant way of spending. Are you ready to return to a real way of purchasing what you need—when you can afford it?

Now, start thinking about your long-term plans—almost everyone wants to retire someday, right? It may not look like your father's retirement of full-time golfing or fishing. It may be creating the opportunity to monetize your true passion.

If you work for a company, find out what workplace retirement plan or plans are available to you and contribute as much as you can. Not only will you be building your nest egg, you will get some short-term benefits as well. Contributions to a qualified retirement plan, like a 401(k), reduce your taxable income up to a certain amount, every year.

Many employers will match their employees' contributions up to a certain percentage—increasing the amount that has the potential to grow for retirement.

If you currently feel behind the 8-ball and don't think saving or investing is "worth-it"—or maybe you are thinking you have waited too long and you can't possibly save enough—doing nothing is certainly not the answer. Every little bit adds up—and it can make a difference. The power of compounding is something you do not want to underestimate.

You should also examine *how* you are saving for retirement. Start thinking of all the sources of income available to you when you retire. Will your savings and investments keep up with inflation? Will you have enough saved to last you through twenty, thirty or more years of retirement?

What are your attitudes toward saving and investing? Your attitude about money and investing can be the *thing* that can get in the way of getting you where you want and need to be financially.

Now that you have identified and prioritized your goals, as well as developed a budget and a plan—let's focus on some fundamentals.

Third—Know the fundamentals of investing. Understanding how the concepts of inflation, taxes, and balance and diversification can affect your investing strategy will help you make more informed investment choices.

Inflation is the first thing people should understand when it comes to investing. The simplest way to sum up inflation is: It reduces the purchasing power of the dollar over time. It is best explained this way: there is a big difference between what one dollar bought you ten years ago and what it will buy you now. It's what our parents are referring to when they talk about the price of a gallon of milk, or a gallon of gas today.

Whatever investment options you use to invest and grow your savings, it should *at least* keep up with inflation. Without this, your dollars will just get eaten away.

Do you understand that *how* you save for retirement is as important as *how much* you save?

One of the keys is taking advantage of as many tax-reducing and tax-deferred options as possible. Take a look at your whole savings picture. Consider reducing your taxable income as much as possible by "maxing out" your employer's 401(k) and your IRA.

When it comes to long-term investing, equities—what most people call the stock market—have historically outperformed cash investments and outpaced inflation and taxes.

You may be among the people today—especially after recent events—who want to shy away from the stock market because you are fearful of the potential for loss. While it is true that the market does have its ups and downs, it has proven itself over the long run.

History has shown there is always a reason to get out of the market. It has also shown just as clearly that staying in is the most profitable course of action. Keep in mind, of course, that past performance is not an indication of future results.

Even investments made on the worst days of the century, ones with the most upheaval, have historically done well over time.

Fourth—Don't do it yourself. A financial professional can help you create an investment portfolio that will help you achieve your financial goals. While there is no doubt you could try the "do-it-yourself" approach, financial professionals have the time, experience, resources and knowledge at their disposal that you just don't have. A financial professional can also help you stick to your plan, even when the market seems shaky.

How do you find the right person for you? Collect referrals from friends and family. Narrow down your list by starting with phone calls to the referred practitioner—explain your situation—ask if that is something they work on. Are you going through a divorce or are you recently widowed? You might want to find a practitioner who can help you navigate your suddenly single lifestyle, someone who will help you make this transition from life with a partner to life without, someone who specifically works with women making this very important transition.

If your instinct says it could be a good fit, set a time to meet with them for an hour consultation. Listen to their philosophy and get an understanding of their compensation structure. Do they do hourly planning only, or do they charge a percentage of assets, or do they work on commission? None of those are wrong, or bad—simply make sure you are comfortable with how they run their business.

A good financial professional should be able to answer any questions you may have and explain the potential risks and rewards associated with various investments or investment products.
If you do have a relationship with an advisor, maybe it has been awhile since you met with them. Pick up the phone and call—

schedule a time for your check-up and be sure to ask:

1. Where do you stand today?
2. Where do you need to be in the future?
3. Does your current portfolio meet your goals and time horizon?

It's never too late. There is always something you can do—ignoring what you have not done for yourself and your finances will not change your current situation.

Whatever financial mistakes you have made in your past—let them go. Today is the beginning of your future—the choices you make will have lasting impact.

I wish for you prosperity and the good fortune you deserve.

Debbie Whitlock is a registered representative of and offers securities through Woodbury Financial Services, Inc. Member FINRA, SIPC, P.O. Box 64284, St. Paul, MN, 55164, 800.800.2638. The opinions of the author do not necessarily reflect those of Woodbury Financial Services, Inc. or its affiliates.

DEBBIE WHITLOCK
President, Sound Financial Partners
Founder, Femme Finance™

Investment strategies for women

(206) 749-5111
debbie@debbiewhitlock.com
www.debbiewhitlock.com
www.soundfinancialpartners.com

For 14 years, Debbie Whitlock has been financially educating and empowering suddenly single women as they make the financial transition from life with a partner to one without. With tremendous compassion and skill, she reminds women that addressing their financial future from scarcity and fear will not lead to the prosperity they desire and deserve. Debbie helps women appreciate that knowledge is power and once you "know" what you don't know—she can provide the tools to understand the foreign language of finance.

Frequently quoted in major print and online publications, including Forbes.com, she is committed to creating a financial revolution for women and investing through education and enrichment.

In 2008, she was recognized by Woodbury Financial Services as Woman of The Year for her work with women and investing.

Debbie is President of Sound Financial Partners, and founder of Femme Finance™. She is a graduate of Washington State University and is licensed to sell securities in the states of Washington, California, Michigan, New York and Massachusetts. Currently, she is pursuing her CFP designation through the American College, and hosts her own weekly syndicated radio program on CBS Radio and the I'm Thankful Network.

Escaping the Prison of Perfection
From Fraud to Fulfilled
By Regena Schwarz Garrepy, CDC, CDCGL, RCS, NLC

I often joke that I am a "recovering perfectionist"—but it's true. My recovery began years ago at an annual checkup at my doctor's office when he simply asked, *"How are you doing?"*

Exposed and vulnerable, I still answered on autopilot. *"Great. Everything is perfect."* In that moment, I could not recognize the sound of my own voice. Even though I looked like a woman who had it all together, I was slowly suffocating and I could not admit it. I felt trapped in my own self-inflicted "Prison of Perfection"—built with invisible walls of ideals, standards and expectations. I achieved everything I had always believed was the "perfect" life, yet I could never relax or enjoy it. I was left feeling exhausted, disconnected, guilty, unfulfilled and worst of all, like a fraud. I was spending hours of my day doing things I hated because I thought those were the activities I *should* be doing. Nothing ever felt "good enough." Perfectionism was also costing me close relationships because I could not ask for help or express how I felt. As I escaped the doctor's office that day, my "Prison of Perfection" breakout began.

As little girls, we believe in fairy tales—those happily-ever-after scenarios that typically include a prince, a magnificent castle and a breathtaking dress for the ball. Even now, we are bombarded with idealized images. We assume that the more perfect the vision, the better the ending and the happier we will be. But this is often a facade, and consequently, many women with wonderful jobs, houses, partners and children end up feeling empty.

Are You an Inmate in the Prison of Perfection?

- Are you surrounded by family and friends, but still feel lonely?

- Do you keep your true feelings to yourself but put on a facade for others?

- Do you ever feel guilty about how you really feel—wondering to yourself, "How dare you be miserable when you have so much?"

- Do you find yourself resentful or overly sensitive when someone offers suggestions or help?

- Do you constantly replay situations or events, fixating on ways you could have done it better?

- Do you obsess over what others—even complete strangers—might think about you?

- Have you found yourself saying, "I don't have time to do it right, so I'm not going to do it at all?"

If you answered "yes" to some of these questions, you may be serving a sentence—without even knowing it.

Escaping the Prison

Happiness does not come from perfection. Escaping the prison by "letting go of perfect" empowers you with the freedom to truly enjoy living the life you have—instead of feeling unsatisfied in the ideal life you keep trying to create. Here are the steps you can take to break out of your "Prison of Perfection" and break through to freedom.

Understand and recognize the perfection filter. Lynn Hargis, founder of Living by Design and a relational communications specialist, describes a filter or screen as a "skewed or clouded vision of self, others, situations and/or circumstances." Our filters are how we make sense of our environment and relate to others. The perfection filter shows up when we begin to view our world through competition and comparisons. A person with a strong perfection filter may be driven to be "better than," often to counteract her core limiting belief of never feeling "good enough."

Perfectionists can also show up as people pleasers—trying to be everything to everyone. When you become stressed or fatigued, your filters are exacerbated. The first step in escaping the "prison of perfection" is recognizing how the perfection filter shows up in your life. Are you often comparing yourself to others? Do you feel driven to be the best or get it exactly right? Do certain tasks seem so overwhelming that you don't bother getting started? Do you put things off because you don't have time to do it the right way? Do you do everything yourself because you cannot trust anyone to do the job as well as you? Begin catching yourself reacting to life through these filters.

Identify what the perfectionist has cost you. In order to be ready and willing to escape the prison, it is important for you to understand exactly what you have given up for your perfectionist. Ask yourself:

- Has the perfectionist denied you a deeper sense of peace because you are always striving for more—and never feeling like what you are doing is enough? Does this leave you feeling overwhelmed and guilty?

- Have you sacrificed your own authenticity or your connection and intimacy with others by doing it all yourself and not asking for help?

- Have you missed opportunities for success because you felt unprepared or inadequate?

- Has your self-trust and decisiveness been forfeited because you were worried about what others would think?

- Have you forgotten how to enjoy the moment, relax and just have fun?

Take a few minutes to reflect—and then I invite you to write down what you have sacrificed because of your perfectionist.

Identify what the perfectionist has given you. While your personal perfectionist can wreak havoc, it has also served you in some capacity. Ask yourself:

- Has your work ethic and attention to detail brought you success?

- Have you been promoted, praised or appreciated due to your extra efforts or focus on quality?

- Are you able to multitask, organize or even handle high-pressure situations?

Your perfectionist is *not* a villain. It may have given you drive and motivation. Which parts of the perfectionist have served you? On the same sheet of paper, write down the benefits of your perfectionist.

Give your perfectionist a promotion. You do not have to kill the perfectionist in order to escape the prison. It has skills and talents that are valuable. Now that you have a clear inventory of those pros and cons, it is time to relieve her of certain duties and highlight others. First, create a list of what your perfectionist is no longer responsible for—like no more obsessing. No more destructive critiquing of yourself and others. No more "martyr syndrome" and doing it all alone. No more competing and comparing to everyone else. No more feeling overwhelmed with guilt.

After you've laid off the perfectionist, evaluate the gifts of the perfectionist and empower it to help you. Promote your perfectionist to the job of "success coach," who lovingly holds you accountable and encourages you to reach for excellence—without the abuse.

Face the fear of leaving the prison. Human beings naturally resist change—even when the change is beneficial. If it were easy to stop being a perfectionist, you would have done so already. At some level you have become comfortable in your habits, and breaking free of them poses risk, doubt and even fear. In my own experience, I have observed that many women take controlled and calculated steps to avoid making mistakes. You begin to edit and rehearse so much that it keeps you from knowing yourself.

Start with small, positive risks. Forget making the bed, or take the night off and eat your favorite dinner on the floor. Ask for help or delegate a duty without micromanaging. Invite your neighbor over for coffee without cleaning your house to "white glove" standards. Do something off the cuff and unrehearsed. Open your heart, lower the wall and trust someone. Face the fear of being found out as "not perfect." Embrace the courage it takes to be authentic and, in doing so, you will find that your vulnerability actually leads to greater self-trust and more meaningful relationships with others.

Finding Fulfillment

Once we step out from behind those invisible bars, a whole new world awaits us. It will take some practice and some patience to appreciate where you now live. Here are some steps to guide you in finding fulfillment for life on the outside of the "Prison of Perfection."

Remember life is a journey—not a competition. Our perfection filters keep us continually comparing and competing, often preventing us from enjoying ourselves. Life is filled with obstacles, but it is combined with glorious experiences along the way. We often get caught up in the "end result." When we are viewing each project, moment and day as something we need to master, we return to the feeling that we are never quite enough. We try harder, we give up, we panic or we berate ourselves for not getting it right. When you feel yourself heading into one of those modes, remember to look around and enjoy the scenery. Celebrate each and every mile marker, not just the finish line.

Stop and breathe. Stress causes physical tension and toxins to build up in the body. Using relaxation techniques like yoga, meditation or breathing exercises can help you refocus and transition out of the perfectionist panic. Try creating a ritual to get centered. Try this: Slow down and release tension from your body. Drop your shoulders. Relax your jaw. Connect the soles of your feet to the ground. Breathe in. Let all the voices in your head get quiet.

Separate what is actually happening versus what you are making up in your mind. Are you stressed because the project is not completed or because you are worried it isn't good enough? Are you panicking because you do not have enough time to make dinner or because you cannot make a certain meal from scratch? Are you upset that your in-laws are stopping over because you don't feel like company, or is it because your bathroom is not clean and the living room is not picked up? Is it really that bad?

Focus on what is really important in the moment. Is it critical that you add an extra chart or additional option to the presentation to put it over the top? Or is it more beneficial that you get some sleep before presenting? Is it more important to enjoy the process of making cupcakes with your daughter or that you alone create the best decorated birthday cake she has ever had? Is it more important to speak your truth with an open heart or to silence yourself by saying what someone wants to hear? In all situations, you have a choice. Ask yourself: *"What is important right now?"*

Act from excellence—not perfection. After we know what is most important, we can respond with care, concern and quality. You can still be successful, polished, professional, hospitable and compassionate while working toward excellence instead of holding onto perfection.

Move into "more than enough." *You have more than enough—and you are more than enough.* Adopt and repeat this mantra. Remember that this is an attitude and a belief that you can choose just as easily as choosing that you are not enough. If struggling with this belief holds you back or makes you feel guilty, these three action steps will help:

1. Honor your own value. You are a unique and special person with distinct skills and talents. Sometimes we are so busy trying to get it all right that we dismiss our own value. Take an inventory of your gifts: are you a compassionate listener? Are you an effective communicator? Do you see the potential in others? Are you artistically creative? Maybe you are musically inclined, can make pantry items into a gourmet meal or have expertise in your career field. Write down your gifts and soak them in, and look for ways to use your value in service to the world. When someone takes the time to give you a sincere compliment or acknowledgement, honor the person and the gesture by being truly receptive, accepting the praise and genuinely thanking them for sharing their feedback. If you dismiss the moment, you can dismiss your value.

2. Recognize your wealth. You have abundance all around you. As we strive and struggle to be more and do more, we are blinded to what we already have. Start noticing all the areas of your life in which you are graced with riches. While in the grocery story or standing in front of your pantry, notice all of the colorful options you have and the delicious abundance of food. Close your eyes and think about the beautiful faces of the people who have come into your life as a friend, teacher, supporter or resource. Look around your home and office and notice all of the ways your life is eased through technology and convenience. Count your skills and knowledge and training as your personal mental wealth. When you hear the voice of your perfectionist chiming in about what you are missing—what you do not have or why you are not enough—turn up the voice of gratitude in appreciation of what you *do* have.

3. Learn the art of surrender. For most people, the word "surrender" conjures up the image of a white flag and the feeling of being defeated and giving up. For a newly escaped perfectionist, the word "surrender" seems to go against everything that is in our nature. I invite you to consider the idea of the butterfly: the caterpillar must let go of what it knows itself to be. The caterpillar surrenders to its process and goes into the unknown in order to emerge as a glorious butterfly. At its deepest level, surrender is not about giving up or being defeated—it is truly about faith.

The art of surrender is about learning to trust yourself and others, and embracing the process of living. Perhaps you are feeling overwhelmed with your demands at home, at work, and within your personal life. At some point, you can either succumb to the stress and anxiety or you can surrender to the idea that you are not perfect. You are "in process" as a human being and you have value. In fact, there is a peaceful freedom in surrendering: it means you don't have to have all the answers and you don't have to be everything for everybody. As you learn the art of surrender, you will become less judgmental of yourself and more compassionate. Eventually, you will realize that you can hold other people capable of making their own choices. You are not responsible for how everyone else looks, feels and thinks. The very act of surrendering is truly "letting go of perfection."

I invite you to step into a world where you can relax, laugh and feel fulfilled—a world where you can connect with others, trust yourself, and feel like you are evolving instead of just achieving. You are *not* perfect—and that's more than okay. You are the glorious, talented, unique *you*. Celebrate your escape and embrace the freedom of truly living your incredible life.

REGENA SCHWARZ GARREPY,
CDC, CDCGL, RCS, NLC
Reclaim Your Essence

(407) 230-4053
regena@reclaimyouressence.com
www.reclaimyouressence.com
www.livingbydesignusa.org

Going from a high-performing educator to a stay-at-home mom to an award-winning direct sales professional, Regena Garrepy knows how scary change can be. She understands first-hand how we can lose touch with parts of ourselves that get lost or abandoned through the challenges and stresses of life. She is passionate about coaching others to reclaim their true essence. She guides clients to reclaim their voice, confidence, power or body—so they can discover a sense of peace, fulfillment and balance.

Regena is a Certified Dream Coach,® Dream Coach Group Leader™ and Trainer through Dream University.® She is also a True Purpose™ Coach and a Relational Communications and Nutritional Lifestyle Coach with Living By Design. As a certified Leadership Instructor with CASA, she volunteers with the Student Leadership Training Program, teaching students to become tomorrow's leaders.

Drawing on her years of experience in education, sales, training and coaching, Regena is also an inspiring speaker and workshop presenter. She has earned top sales, top recruiting and leadership recognition within her direct sales company and leads a team of consultants from across the United States.

Regena finds great joy in family, food and yoga. *Namaste!*

The Embodiment of Integrity
The Secret to Personal Power and Fulfillment
By Jennifer Mayfield, MPA

Happiness is when what you think, what you say,
and what you do are in harmony.
—Mahatma Gandhi, peace activist

*M*any people seek the quick fix to success, manifestation or a life full of joy. I have a secret to share with you: personal power and fulfillment lie in living a life of integrity, a life that is pure of heart. There is no quick fix to get there; the answer lies in knowing who it is you want to be in the world, declaring it, honing the actions you take to create it and then pursuing a life guided by integrity with devoted and crystal focus. This all starts with building a relationship with your own heart.

If you want to discover a pathway to lightheartedness, clarity, vitality, serenity and love—for yourself first and from there you will have a cupful for others—integrity will take you there. This path is not for the faint of heart. It requires a willingness to stand in the face of the storm if necessary, trusting that on the other side is the sweet experience of feeling bathed by the storm showers, and drinking in the light from the emerging sun. Life becomes a playground of effortless self-effort.

This chapter offers you practices to become more intimate with your personal integrity. If you want to bring joy, connection and power into your life, this chapter will provide practices to support you. You will learn how to develop the ability to be with what is so, and when the moment comes, to choose powerfully to take action. Imagine living your life 90 percent of the time in integrity, experiencing a life that looks and feels on the outside what you envision on the inside. From this place of whole and complete freedom, what would you be doing? Who would you be?

I am defining integrity *as living a life that honors your commitments and is aligned with the truth of your heart.* What an exciting possibility! Through discovery of your personal commitments and acting within them, life naturally falls into alignment. When you are in harmony, there is a sense of unity within and without. You are the embodiment of integrity.

Often, new coaching clients come to me with lives that are "wonky." I immediately check in with them about their integrity. I invite them to create an Integrity Checklist where they write down all of the areas where their actions are not in alignment with their words and thoughts. The idea is to create a list that touches all areas of their lives, and ranges from "eating more vegetables," to "breaking up with my long-term lover" as places to look. We lovingly and ruthlessly root out as much as we can that is not in alignment. Then, the invitation is to get on task, checking the list off. A few check marks later and my clients report experiencing serenity, surges of power and days that are more easeful.

How about you? I invite you to take the time to create your own list. Take a moment and write down anywhere in your life that you are aware that your actions are not in alignment with what you value and what you are thinking and saying.

In the long term, I work closely with my coaching clients to discover what it is they really want in life. It may sound easy, but as you begin to practice making commitments in life, you may discover what so many of my clients discover: that sometimes they get what they said they wanted and they didn't really want it. It could be years of schooling to become an attorney, only to discover they did it for their parents. Or saving enough money to purchase a new couch and a few days later, the thrill is gone. Or it could be taking time to volunteer, then realizing that their work with the charity is not as fulfilling as expected. There are layers of unlearning, and practicing stepping into discovery of what is at the heart of their desires for themselves. When they gain clarity, they can be effective in creating whatever they want for themselves and others as well; they can be a true contribution to the world.

Integrity Invites Radical Honesty with Yourself

Integrity is being certain about what your heart most wants in the moment. For starters, it is a good idea to become familiar with those parts of you that stand in the way of you knowing your heart. In general, they will be those disowned parts of you that operate unconsciously to keep you small. Begin to notice how you sabotage yourself, how you practice negativity or when you react rather than respond. Did you eat a second donut even though you say you are committed to watching your sugar intake? Do you take loved ones for granted, even though you say family is most important? Do you have a secret wish to learn to fly an airplane but keep putting everyone else's desire before your own? Have you told yourself you would go to an event you were really looking forward to, then didn't get off the Internet soon enough to be on time? Take a moment right now to take three long deep breaths. Now ask yourself:

"What are my secrets, dark parts or stories I tell myself to justify my actions?"

Then ask yourself:
"From what part of myself am I disconnected?"

Are you disconnected from the playful child you used to be, or did you find a deep well of anger or grief that you keep trying to force down inside you? These are fragmented parts of yourself that muddy your clarity in taking action in your life. Take time to be with these parts of yourself, befriend them. Then when they show up to veil your heart's true knowledge of itself you will be able to discern them.

Discerning your heart's desire is the flip side of befriending your shadow—that darker side of ourselves we all have. As you are more willing to reach into the darker areas of yourself—your envy, your disappointment—the more you are able to experience acceptance, compassion and other lighter emotions. When you can be with buried grief, you can then create more joy. Integrity loves—and is—balance and expansion. When your being is in perfect union, the heart responds by expressing itself more purely. You become closer to the heart's true longings and attuned to its guidance. This kind of radical honesty with yourself compliments the next practice, meditation.

Get to Know Your Own Self through Meditation

Turning inward again and again is a practice that all great spiritual teachers have offered throughout history. Meditation brings us to the space of the heart, and supports every aspect of daily life. Some of its benefits related to integrity are clarity, serenity, centeredness and presence. If you choose only one practice from this chapter, I recommend meditation. Meditation is an act of love and honor for yourself and others. Your life of integrity begins with a simple ten-minute-a-day meditation practice, five days a week.

1. Sit comfortably and focus on a mantra, or the words "I am love," or another phrase that is meaningful for you.

2. Breathe your words inward to the heart space; breathe your words out from the heart space.

Once you begin you may experience thoughts, and emotions may arise. Just notice them, allow them to drift by like clouds, and return to your mantra or words and the breath. The more you meditate, the easier it will get and the more aware you will become of your personal truth.

Align Your Thoughts and Actions with Your Commitments

Begin to practice noticing your thoughts even before they are fully formed, and discover whether they are in alignment with your heartfelt commitments. If they are not, it is possible, with focused practice, to release the initial thought and therefore not act. Bring awareness to your thoughts with these practices:

1. Notice when a thought arises, and from where.

2. In what part of your body do you experience your thoughts?

3. Can you discover the experience of letting thoughts go that do not serve you?

One of my commitments is authentic love and connection. I am separated from my husband, but when we were together, I sometimes felt a pang in my belly when I would think, "We should go to the movies." Those times when I felt a pang, if I suggested a movie anyway, I was ignoring a signal to create connection in another way and was not fulfilling my commitment to authentic love. On the other hand, integrity might have looked like a suggestion for an intimate dinner before the movie, or an early movie with time for connection through sexual intimacy afterwards.

1. Remember a time when you experienced an inner signal that

what you were planning or doing was not in alignment with your commitment.

2. What happened when you listened to the signal? Or, what happened when you didn't?

3. When you listened to the signal, what was the outcome of your action? What did that provide you? Peace? Joy? A surge of energy?

4. Or, if you didn't follow the signal, contemplate what it cost you to disregard it. How could you have been and acted differently? For example, could you feel your face getting red, but you shouted at the food server anyway? What if you took a deep breath, and from a commitment to play, cracked a joke instead?

Practice Flexibility within Your Commitments

Sometimes the path to your commitment takes an unexpected turn, calling for the skill of flexibility. It is an acknowledgment of the possibility for taking a straight path, or a curved path toward your commitment. Both ways are valid. Checking in with your heart again and again, listening deeply and acting responsibly on what you learn, is an act of honoring yourself and others.

Here's a classic example: You are out shopping and run into an acquaintance and say, "We should get together . . . " Did you say the preceding with a downward intonation filled with the spirit of good intention that just is not going to happen? Where is the integrity in this cliché? Without flexibility, it's a win/lose: either you get together or you don't. When you practice checking in, you allow for a change of heart. There is an invitation for radical honesty with yourself and others, therefore creating a win/win. How about, "Wow! It's great to see you! I have the impulse to say let's get together, but knowing how busy I am, I won't follow through." Or, "I am so glad to see you. When is a good time to chat by phone or get together?" Or, "When

I see you I realize how many times I've said 'Let's get together.' How about we get some coffee right now?" Or, "Hi, great to see you. Bye."

There may be places in your life where you operate with total integrity and there may be other places in your life where you may not be in full integrity. Some places to look are with your family, friends, job, merchants, neighbors and volunteer organizations.

1. Is there anything you said to someone recently that you have not followed up on?

2. Brainstorm other possible steps to accomplish the same outcome.

3. Take one action today to shift who you are being about the situation. Have you a sense of foreboding regarding that email you said you would send? Or that call you would make or that cake for the charity sale you said you would bake?

4. In addition, take one action to experience integrity in that area of your life. Perhaps, you are overcommitting, or saying "yes" when you really want to say "no," or trying to be two places at once so you do not have to choose what is the best use of your time.

I recall once telling my ten-year-old son, "We should go to that Chinese restaurant you like so much, just the two of us." Then I noticed that weeks passed, I kept meaning to go, but still no trip to the restaurant. I was out of integrity with myself, and my child: I had a thought, articulated it, but no action. To return to integrity, I set up a specific "by when" I would go to the restaurant with my son. We later scheduled our dinner date, and since then we have a regular rhythm of dates when the two of us spend special time together.

Integrity Is a Whole Body Experience

Imagine the amount of energy it takes to juggle unfulfilled declarations in your mind. Your declarations could be things like, "I am going to call my brother weekly," or "I am going to choose a form of exercise that is fun and do it!" or "I am going to give 10 percent of what I earn to charity." Each of those unfulfilled intentions is like a pinprick in your subtle body. Other examples are every time you say, "Yes, I'll do that," when you do not mean it or think "I can't tell that person what I really think or feel, because they might get upset or hurt, or hurt me." When you do this, you create personal power leaks.

Power leaks in the body mean that vitality, joy and ease are fleeting. As you step into living a life of conscious integrity, supporting the body will serve you well. Ask yourself, "What would support me in caring for my body on all levels?" Make a list. Your list might include bodywork, exercise, eating right, a support group, watching a favorite comedy or life coaching. Creating a healthy body in which personal integrity can dwell will support the other actions you take to be in integrity, and sustain power and fulfillment in your life.

Integrity Is About Refreshing Your Commitments

With clear commitments, and continued renewal and reflection on them, you bring focus and power to your life. As I said previously, so many times in life we get what we want and we discover it isn't really what we wanted. Therefore, it is important to take an intimate look at whatever you are up to. Over time, you will develop the capacity to maintain single-minded focus on those activities that are most congruent with your commitments. I invite you to practice radical integrity with yourself first, building a solid connection with both the feminine and masculine self that is your true nature.

1. Write down your top seven commitments.

2. Set aside a time to reconnect with your commitments daily, for example, before you go to sleep or get up in the morning.

Daily reflection and refreshment of your commitments is a grounding practice—it keeps you connected to what is really important to you in your life. This is also a great time to practice gratitude and blessings.

You Can Embody Integrity

One of my friends and my son's beloved teacher, Tara Kintz, shared the following when I told her about this chapter. She said, "Where did it (integrity) go? You never had it, integrity is not fixed—it is a moment by moment phenomenon." Integrity is about conscious awareness, being with what is your truth, compassion for yourself where you are, and the knowledge that you always have the choice to return to integrity.

In practicing the renewed paradigm of embodied integrity, there is a return to wholeness—a unity of all parts of yourself. You experience it through living your everyday life, witnessing your tendencies and redirecting your attention to your heart's highest calling. You are harmonized. It is not just something you do; it is who you are being. You can't take on your own precious gift of being human without turning toward the heart, listening intently and acting from there. By honoring wherever you are, as the layers of what clouds you from knowing your heart continue to lift through your dedicated practices, you are giving yourself, others and the planet an opportunity to heal into the power that you and the planet always have.

Now, choose to listen to your heart and follow its guidance. The value of listening to your heart is a life of integrity that is personal power and joy. Embodying integrity honors your commitments and empowers you, in every moment, to live your authentic life.

JENNIFER MAYFIELD, MPA
Inspirational Speaker & Author,
Group, Personal and Executive Life Coach

Inspiring to make a difference

(510) 847-9744
jennifer@jennifermayfield.com
www.jennifermayfield.com

Jennifer Mayfield, MPA, has worked in multinational corporations, nonprofits and the public sector for over a dozen years. She is also a devoted spiritual student. The essence of her work is expanding each individual's inherent intelligence through group and one-on-one coaching. She is an expert at guiding clients to recognize and integrate their current skills, knowledge and talents with their deeper wisdom. Her work, whether one-on-one or in an energy-filled workshop, is on the cutting edge of personal and organizational change.

Jennifer's heart-centered coaching presence, powerful leadership and educational background generates lively and lasting results. With Jennifer, you can expect to laugh, get on task, be inspired and connect with a deeper knowledge that will bring you or your organization further into alignment with current trends. Jennifer is an inspirational leader, and a coach and a trainer for leaders and coaches. Jennifer received a Bachelor of Arts in Community Studies with a focus on alternative organizations and a Master's Degree in Public Administration. She is a member of the International Coaching Federation and a graduate of the world-class Accomplishment Coaching Coaches' Training Program. Creative, illuminating and down to earth, Jennifer's warmth and enthusiasm is felt whether she is at a Little League baseball game with her kids or speaking in a room filled with successful business owners and executives.

True Joy Is an Inside Job
Simple Steps to Uncovering Your Essential Joy
By Catherine Ewing-Rinker, LCSW, MDiv, RMT, CDC

"Joy does not simply happen to us.
We have to choose joy and keep choosing it every day."
—Henri Nouwen, Dutch priest, author and professor

*M*any of us have experienced fleeting moments of joy. The birth of a child, the sight of a beautiful sunset or the embrace of a lover can invoke feelings of ecstasy, bliss or delight that we identify as joy. Recent studies tell us that few American adults report feeling joy or happiness as a regular part of their life experience, however. According to the Harris Interactive Study, released in 2005, only 20 percent of American adults feel ongoing joy or fulfillment. Those fleeting moments are far outweighed by feelings of anxiety, depression and overwhelming obligation. Life feels more like a series of "shoulds" and "have tos," accompanied by an aching sense that "there has got to be something more." In my practice as a psychotherapist, coach and healer, I hear this refrain day in and day out. It saddens me to see how many people experience this in their lives.

The good news is that it is possible to experience joy as a consistent internal state of well-being rather than a random, fleeting occurrence dependent on outside circumstances. Helping people to understand that joy is a conscious choice, a state of being that each of us has the ability to create and sustain is an integral part of my work. Creating a life of joy is an inside job. It takes work and requires developing a relationship with all parts of your Self: mental, emotional, physical and spiritual.

Choosing joy clears the way for miracles. As we explore the aspects of Self and their relationship to joy, you will begin to understand this statement more deeply. It is not simply a nice sounding cliché, it is a fact supported by the fields of neuropsychology, quantum physics, energy medicine and spiritual truth. The implications of consciously choosing joy are significant not only for each individual but for the entire world community.

Multiple Aspects of Self

During his initial visit with me, a new client promptly handed me a list of his many illnesses and medications. Trust me when I tell you that it was a very long list, and that he is not the first client to have done that. Sadly, it tells me that people often define themselves as little more than their illnesses, surgeries and medications. This is their "story" and they unknowingly reinforce it every time they repeat it to themselves or to another person. They are usually surprised when I thank them for the list and put it in their file, unread. Then I talk to them about their different Selves: mental, emotional, physical and spiritual, and how these Selves are energetically linked to each other. Unknowingly, by focusing on their problems they are actually digging the neural pathways of their dis-ease ever deeper. The gentleman I mentioned earlier walked into his session recently and announced that, in an "ah-ha" moment, he had realized that every time he'd experienced a loss in his life he had developed another illness. The light bulb had gone off: he had made the connection between his thoughts, emotions and the physical manifestations of illness in his body and his deeply depleted spirit. Let's look in more detail at how the various aspects of our Selves work in partnership with each other.

The Mental Body

The brain is the primary organ of the mental body and is most closely associated with the Ego. It has two primary tasks: survival and organization. Of these two, survival is more critical and our minds will do whatever it takes to keep us fitting in and protected. On a primitive level, this makes perfect sense; you did not survive long if you were not part of the tribe. What does that mean for us modern-day humans?

It is a commonly accepted fact in the field of personal development that human adults have approximately 70,000 thoughts a day; nearly 95 percent are repetitive and 80 percent are fearful or negative. The mind does not differentiate between what you imagine and what actually exists in your outer world. If it "sees" something, even if it exists only in your imagination, it responds as though it is real. It responds to your thoughts in the same way. Fearful or anxious thoughts represent some perceived danger and may result in the body taking on the fight or flight response, ready to run or defend itself. No wonder so many of us feel frazzled and exhausted. What can you do to break free of this cycle or worry and physiological response?

The first step is to realize that you are not your thoughts. You are a spiritual being with an essence of pure love. Your thoughts are mental constructs taken on from other people and institutions. They have nothing to do with the truth of who you are. Once you realize this and begin to see your thoughts as being outside of yourself, you take back your power over these "mental delinquents." Then you can begin to exercise choice over which thoughts you will allow into your head and which you will reject. If a thought is not helpful or supportive, toss it out and choose a new one. Each time you become aware of an old thought creeping back in, choose to replace it with a new, empowering thought. This takes consistent practice, but over time you will notice the positive effects in your life.

I believe the most important step is to release old limiting beliefs that are running your life at a subconscious level. Beliefs are simply thoughts that have been thought over and over again, becoming solidified into a rigid set of rules that run your life without you even knowing it. Much like a computer, old beliefs are like an outdated software program that will keep you responding the same way until you consciously choose a different response. You continue to react to present moment events from your past programming until you pull out the old software and insert a new, updated version of yourself! In my years of working with clients, I have realized that it is not enough to talk about these ideas to fully release their grip. After all, they are subconscious and the mind only knows what the mind knows. These beliefs are held in your cellular memory, and they must be released at that level if you are going to experience real, long-lasting change. There are many different ways to release limiting beliefs, including Emotional Freedom Technique, Neuro Emotional Technique, Energy Healing and The Work.

Next, it is necessary to become clear about the things you wish to be, do or have in your life. Everything that exists in physical form existed first as a thought in someone's mind. It is impossible to create the things in your life that will bring you joy if you do not know what those things are. Begin to explore what you are passionate about, what makes your heart sing, what you do just for the love of it. *The Passion Test,* written by Janet and Chris Attwood and published by Penguin Group in 2007, is a great process to get you thinking about what you want to create in your life.

According to The Law of Attraction, everything is energy and like energy attracts like energy. Whatever you put your attention on, consistently and with feeling, eventually shows up in your life. For many people, their thoughts are focused on the things that they don't want or don't have. This scientific law responds to the energy, the vibrational frequency of your thoughts, not the words themselves. It does not hear the "don't" when you say "I don't want to be sick" or "I don't want to be in debt." It picks up the vibration of your thought and simply returns to you more of what you are thinking or vibrating about. Whether your attention is on what you want or what you don't want, you will receive exactly that! Begin to consciously put your attention on those things that will bring out the joy that is already inside of you.

The Emotional Body

Since childhood, you have received all kinds of messages about emotions and what to do with them. Emotions are labeled as good or bad, acceptable or not—often depending on your gender. Emotional people are considered to be sick or weak and needing to learn to toughen up and deal with life. You are rarely given permission to feel and explore your emotions and what they may have to teach you. The truth is that emotions are simply *energy in motion;* neither good nor bad, right nor wrong. They are signals, clues about the circumstances in your life and whether those circumstances are aligned with your true desires and who you are as a spiritual being. We are all meant to stop resisting, to feel our emotions fully, to tune into the messages they are sending, and to take responsibility for making the changes necessary to bring ourselves back into a more balanced and joyful state.

When working with clients to identify and release emotions, I often ask them to close their eyes, go into a relaxed state and notice where in their body they may be feeling a particular emotion. Then I ask them to have a conversation with that body part, asking questions such as, "What emotion(s) am I feeling?" or "When have I felt like this before?" Or "How old do I feel?" Or, "What does this emotion have to tell me?" This allows the client to get at subconscious information stored in the body and to gain a better understanding of their emotional state.

All of this is done from a place of non-judgment, as a neutral observer of the information that comes forth. Once the client receives the information, whatever it may be, I ask them to thank the body for sharing its wisdom and to stay open for any additional information that may be forthcoming.

Following this expression of gratitude I then invite my client to ask whether there are any limiting beliefs connected to the emotions. For most people, this opens up a Pandora's Box of hurt, shame and unworthiness, to name a few. Then we go to work dismantling those limiting beliefs. I find that Energy Psychology, especially the Emotional Freedom Technique, is the best way to clear out these limiting beliefs and the associated emotions. Developing this relationship with your emotional self and making a commitment to feel and explore your emotions is perhaps the greatest step you can take toward living a life of greater authenticity and joy.

The Physical Body

From an energetic perspective, this is the densest of our bodies. Consequently, it is the last place where the evidence of your thoughts and emotions shows up. But have no doubt—it will show up! From mild aches and pains to full-blown disease, the physical body will eventually reveal the negative energy stored in the cells of your body. As I mentioned earlier, negative thoughts and related emotions put your body into fight or flight response. In this state of heightened alertness, the body experiences a number of physiological responses, including increased adrenaline flow, accelerated heart and lung action, muscle contraction and constricted blood flow. While useful in a real crisis, repeated and prolonged stress responses may result in chronic suppression of the immune system, leaving the body open to infection and illness. If your thoughts tend to be negative, worried or anxious, you are planting the seeds of serious physical dis-ease.

Symptoms in the physical body are always clues to what is going on in your mental and emotional bodies. Your core beliefs and your thoughts about illness and aging will significantly impact your overall physical well-being. Your physical body is the temple for your Soul. Caring for it through healthy lifestyle choices and paying attention to the messages it can convey is a piece of the puzzle of joy. I recommend Louise Hay, Caroline Myss and Dr. Joan Borysenko, mind/body/spirit experts, as excellent resources for helping to understand the connection between unresolved emotions, negative mental constructs and manifestations of illness and disease in the physical body. Louise Hay's book, *Heal Your Body,* published by Hay House in 1984, includes an alphabetical chart of physical ailments, the probable causes, and healing affirmations to help you eliminate old patterns. In *Anatomy of the Spirit,* published by Three Rivers Press in 1997, Carolyn Myss offers a stunning picture of the human body's hidden energetic structures, revealing the relationships between the seven chakras, the mental/emotional imbalance and the possible physical manifestations of imbalance. Based on Dr. Borysenko's work at the Mind/Body Clinic in Boston, her book, *Minding the Body, Mending the Mind* published by Da Capo Press in 2007, contains tips on how to elicit the mind's powerful relaxation response to boost your immune system, cope with chronic pain and alleviate symptoms of a host of stress-related illnesses.

The Spiritual Body

"Joy is not in things, it is in us."
—Richard Wagner, German composer and theorist

I use the term "Spiritual Body" here to refer to the Soul or Higher Self, the part of you that is eternally connected to the Divine Creative Source. Perhaps you have heard the phrase, "you are a Spiritual Being having a human experience." This speaks to your basic essence as an extension of the creative force of the Universe, a unique spark of eternal being-ness. Beginning to think of yourself in this way, rather than as a mortal human being, can profoundly impact your experience of joy. Joy is part of who you are, deep within, part of your birthright as a spiritual being. Rather than something you get from external events or experience, joy is something you find within yourself as you connect with your emotions, release limiting beliefs, honor your physical body and recognize your true nature.

There are many personal practices that will help you connect with your spiritual self, including meditation and prayer, journaling, being in nature, reading inspirational material, yoga and other forms of movement. All of these require the same basic thing: slowing down, getting quiet and intending to hear the still, small voice inside that is so hard to hear over the din of everyday life. With commitment and practice you will be able to connect more easily with the spirit within you and have this eternal, loving presence begin to guide your thoughts, words and actions.

Perhaps the most important and easiest spiritual practice is to begin expressing gratitude and appreciation each day. Start with a few minutes in the morning or evening, perhaps writing in your journal and then gradually increase your expressions throughout your day. Eventually, you will find yourself expressing gratitude not only for the many gifts in your life but also for the challenges, as you begin to see them as opportunities for growth and spiritual mastery.

Joy Heals

"Sometimes your joy can be the source of your smile,
but sometimes your smile can be the source of your joy."
—Thich Nhat Hanh, Vietnamese monk, activist and writer

Sometimes even the simplest task can feel so daunting that you might give up before you start, even if it is something you want. I lovingly invite you to find a few simple ways to bring more joy into your life. Smile as you answer the phone, clean your house or write your bills, sending your body the message that you are relaxed and happy. Find reasons to laugh, celebrate, be light-hearted and notice life's beauty. Smile from your heart as you affirm, "I am joy and it radiates in and through every cell of my body." Your body will respond to the shift in your vibration. Research in neuropsychology and cellular biology now show that our DNA changes when we shift, even momentarily, from anxiety, despair and overwhelm into gratitude, appreciation and joy. Moment by moment you are bringing more light into your cells and raising your energetic vibration. And, since energy attracts like energy, your life will start to become a reflection of this new vibration.

Choosing joy is truly an inside job with profound implications for yourself and our world. Spiritual teacher Mahatma Gandhi tells us, "You must be the change you want to see in the world." Without a doubt, your decision to choose joy in each moment will help bring about a more loving and peaceful world. Creating a life of joy is your conscious choice.

CATHERINE EWING-RINKER, LCSW, MDiv, RMT, CDC

Release your past, ignite your future

(860) 871-9295
catherine@reawakenyourdreamer.com
www.reawakenyourdreamer.com
www.spiritmattersct.com

Catherine, a lifelong student of the mind/body/spirit connection, is a Certified Dream Coach,® Passion Test Facilitator, Psychotherapist, Minister of Spiritual Peacemaking and Reiki Master Teacher. She is also an author, workshop leader, speaker and founder of Spirit Matters, LLC, a holistic healing center. Working with both individuals and groups, Cathy supports those who may be experiencing life transition or searching for greater purpose, authenticity and joy. She is passionate about helping people release old traumas, beliefs and emotions that keep them feeling stuck and unfulfilled. She reconnects clients to their true spiritual nature, allowing them to step out of their story and into a life of passion and purpose.

Catherine's unique combination of professional training, life experience, personality and passion provides a strong platform from which to help clients move to new levels of self-awareness, personal growth and inner peace. Cathy brings her depth of knowledge, wisdom and experience to each person with whom she works. With a broad understanding of spiritual and metaphysical principles and a wide variety of practical tools and resources, Cathy has exactly what it takes to work with each client compassionately and effectively.

From Fear to Freedom
Commit to Change
By Kim Crumpler

"Do you want to be free?
Lift your chains I hold the key.
All power on Heav'n and Earth belong to me.
You are free."
"Set Me Free" from *Lifesong* by Casting Crowns (audio CD, 2005)

"**I**t is time to purge the residual brokenness from your heart, I am ushering you into a new freedom." This message was impressed upon me as I sat prostrate in prayer one Saturday morning, tears rolling down my face. A romance gone sideways had triggered anxiety and a fear that sent me back into old patterns of coping, and questioning my value and my worth This setback became the catalyst for a two-and-a-half-year journey I call, "From Fear to Freedom."

How do you experience personal freedom, a life absent from daily fear, worry and anxiety? Is it really possible to live an incredible life? I say yes, it is possible. No matter your age or personal history, it is never too late to choose to create your incredible life. My desire is that you will find hope in the following reflections and be inspired to begin living without fear.

This journey is not for the faint-hearted. As you travel, think short sprints, then rest and rejuvenate. To help you succeed, get your checklist in order. It is essential to set the framework and pack the right supplies to help strengthen your commitment to change even when you get stuck.

From Fear to Freedom to Be Authentically You

As an infant in the early 1970s, I was adopted into a white family of six. I am African-American and Japanese and, since I lived in a mostly Caucasian community and often experienced prejudice and judgment, I never truly felt okay with who I was. Consistently, there were hurtful reminders that I did not fit in with the black or white communities; I always felt "different." And I certainly was neither comfortable nor confident in my own skin.

My parents divorced when I was six, and my dad left me behind to live with my mom, while most of my siblings lived with my dad and his new family. My self-esteem dropped even more, I grew up in poverty, and I became overweight. My feeling of not being comfortable in my own skin continued to compound, and being unlovable was a key message I held onto as I grew into adulthood. How did this fear that I was never going to be good enough manifest throughout my life? From teenage suicidal thoughts, to depression, to choosing toxic relationships, fear gripped me often. Take a moment to reflect on how fear may have manifested itself in your life in the past or right now.

Today, with commitment to healing childhood wounds and choosing to live in the now, my path from fear to freedom taught me to be proud of who I am. I live comfortably and confidently in my own skin, have a stronger sense of belonging, and I now live in the freedom of being authentically who I was created to be—quirks and all!

Action Steps to Being Your Authentic Self

"Know, first, who you are; and then adorn yourself accordingly."
—Epictetus, Greek philosopher

Give yourself permission to be different. Stop comparing yourself to others. No one else is like you. When you know who you are authentically and give yourself permission to "be," you naturally feel more comfortable and confident in your own skin and allow others the freedom to do the same.

• What skills, talents and abilities do you possess that distinguish you from others?

• What are you passionate about? The arts? Rock climbing? Helping others?

• What personality trait(s) or physical attribute(s) do you most admire about yourself?

Exploring who you are at the core authentically is empowering, creative and liberating. Even if you discover things about yourself of which you are not proud, it's okay. It means you can choose to change if you truly want to.

Dress your authentic self from the inside out. Once you give yourself permission to be you, dress to reflect your authentic self. You may still have a tendency to want to dress like everyone else, but I encourage you to dress as an expression of who you are from the inside out. As a pre-teen, I learned to make a dollar go far at the thrift store. Standing in front of the mirror, I would identify my style likes and dislikes and what colors and cuts best flattered my hard-to-dress shape. I would create unique outfits that reflected my personality, and when I looked like me, I felt great from the inside out; it was magical. When you step into shoes that you love or slip into a dress that embodies your favorite colors, textures and styles, you affirm your unique statement of style, tend to operate from the strength of your core and attract so much more out of life! Through this experience, I was compelled to start Uniquely Savvy, Inc. a personal style and branding company. Through my work, I passionately help others bring down their walls and step into their authentic essence and style from the inside out.

From Fear To Freedom To Forgive

Lack of forgiveness stems from fear that we will get hurt again, fear that we will not be heard or believed, fear that the wrongdoer will not take responsibility, fear of being taken advantage of. The truth is, whether or not someone takes responsibility for his or her actions, we can choose to forgive and release the need for retribution.

I am not suggesting you stay in a situation or relationship that is unhealthy, but channel the time and energy you use to replay the wrong, conjure retaliation and hold pain, into more positive endeavors. If you do not forgive and unlock the keys to the prison that holds the wrongdoer, your lack of forgiveness also jails you.

Is this hard? Absolutely. Can it be done? Absolutely, and when you do, you are empowered to begin the healing process; fear, anger and self-protection begin to dissipate, and you can now move toward being free.

For years, I did not forgive my dad for leaving me behind at age six. As an adult, I chose to do my work around this and set him free from my resentment. Dad made amends, I now have a better understanding of him and myself, and we have a much healthier relationship.

Action Steps to Forgiveness

"Sincere forgiveness isn't colored with expectations that the other person apologize or change. Don't worry whether or not they finally understand you. Love them and release them. Life feeds back truth to people in its own way and time—
just like it does for you and me."
—Sara Paddison, author

Accept that people are not perfect. Sometimes people act from their own pain, fear and experience. When someone is being hurtful toward you, choose to investigate the reason behind the behavior. Often, you will find the motivation was fear and self-protection. While this does not excuse wrong behavior or give license to hurt people, it provides perspective and perhaps a measure of grace to forgive.

Get rid of toxic relationships and set healthy boundaries. Boundaries are designed to keep love in, not out, and they help with forgiveness. Consider what healthy behavior looks and feels like ahead of time so you know when someone, or a group or organization, is toxic. Look at your relationships. Are they rich with mutual respect and reciprocity? Is the relationship built on trust and honesty? You may currently have toxic relationships that require evaluation in your journey toward personal freedom. Be aware that as you choose healthy boundaries, the nature of some relationships is likely to change or even cease. Keep steady. Eventually, choosing healthier relationships from the onset will become your new norm.

"There is only one happiness in life—to love and to be loved."
—George Sand, French novelist

From Fear to Freedom to Love and Be Loved

During the separation from my ex-husband, I started my own very-much-needed recovery. The process was gut-wrenching, isolating, and lonely. I was at a fork in the road with the course of my life, and I had a choice to make. Either I face my past and my fears or I put on my running shoes which would take me miles away from personal growth and freedom.

The breakup of my marriage became the catalyst to find the answer to the soul's question, "Am I lovable?"

Today, I know I am lovable and worthy of being loved. Not because of accolades earned or lofty behavior.

• I am lovable because I am wonderfully made by my Creator.

• I am lovable because I am a good person with a compassionate heart.

• I am lovable because I am loving and committed to loving others well.

Take a few moments to reflect on all the reasons why you are lovable. On a sheet of paper, write, "I am lovable because . . ." List every reason you can think of, then believe it and intentionally live out of that place of truth.

An Action Step to Love and Be Loved

Let others in. Perhaps you have created a fortress around yourself so no one can get to your inner places and hurt you. The problem is that nobody can get in to love you either. The walls are just too thick.

Consider chiseling away one brick at a time with a safe friend who cares about you. My soul sister, Kristin Brown, showed me selfless, genuine love during the darkest times in my adult life. At first, I barely let her in. I did not believe I was lovable, so how could she love and care about me? I was bundled in fear and shame. Her small acts of kindness, from inviting me to share a meal, to listening to my stories without judgment, to providing a sense of family by sharing hers, she taught me what love looked like and how to receive it. Though I did not have a whole lot to offer, she genuinely cared about me—no tricks required. Out of that place of feeling loved and cared for, I began to let my guard down and found I, too, could extend love.

Have you created a fortress around yourself so no one will hurt you? Let down your guard and allow others in—you will find that people genuinely want to love you, too.

Checklist for the Freedom Journey

"If you run, you might lose.
If you don't run, you're guaranteed to lose."
—Jesse Jackson, American civil rights activist and Baptist minister

Begin with the end in mind. What do you really want your freedom life to look like? Do you want to be free from the aching feeling that you are all alone? Free from the fear of failure? Free from the fear that you are just not enough? What do you want to be free from? Write it down.

Determine your core values. When your values are clear, your decisions are easy because your values act as a compass for decision-making. One way to determine your values is to consider what you are willing to fight or pay for and where you are you willing to spend your time and energies. Answering the following questions can help you begin to identify your core values.

- What do you spend your money on—luxury purchases, travel, personal development?

- What do you spend your time on—entertainment, online activities, building relationships?

• What are you willing to fight for—friendship, freedom, a pay increase?

Put a safety net in place. Why? To give you a sense of security when you are being courageous. A safety net is something or someone you can count on to catch you if you fall. It is that extra measure of comfort that propels you to move into risky action. A supportive friend or counselor is a safety net, knowing you can redo something if you make a mistake is another. An open door to have your old job back is yet another safety net. The biggest reason I could confidently choose to face my fears is because of my faith in God. I believed that no matter how stormy the waters would get, He was committed to keeping me afloat. Who or what is your safety net?

Travel light. You will need grace, courage, forgiveness, commitment and gratitude, but leave extra baggage behind. Let bygones be gone and do not think you have to fight every battle that comes your way. A spirit of forgiveness travels more lightly than hard-heartedness and resentment.

Choose the right travel companions. Surround yourself with supportive, positive people who sincerely want you to succeed. Read books and magazines that offer new perspectives and discover possibilities that are brighter than our fearful minds allow us to believe. Find a good church, organization, coach or mentor to help you find your way.

Your mentors do not have to be people you have met. As a latchkey kid dealing with a lot of confusion and adversity, my childhood virtual mentor became Oprah. She overcame her childhood adversities to become an articulate, successful black woman. I thought, "If this woman could do it, so could I." Oprah became my example of what could be. With perseverance, commitment and desire, I, too, could be empowered to rise above my circumstances and create a meaningful life, one step at a time.

With a handful of true friends and trusted advisors, I am blessed to say I am on course. Who are the positive and supportive people and mentors in your life? Do you need to look for some genuine companions to join you on your freedom journey?

Commit to "Yes," Lift Your Chains and Be Free

It is possible to live a new life of hope and freedom, absent from consistent fear and anxiety. I am living proof. Commit today and say "yes" to your freedom journey, lift your chains and be free! Be inspired to be your authentic self, extend forgiveness and learn to love and be loved.

- Celebrate your authentic essence and style every day.

- Extend forgiveness to those who have hurt you.

- Spend your energy on positive endeavors and shun the negative.

- Step into the freedom to love and be loved.

- Look for soulful experiences that cannot be had alone.

- Make personal freedom your new norm.

- Live intentionally, love fully and explore the possibilities of what this incredible life has to offer.

Taking just one baby step today is far less risky than living immobilized by fear for the rest of your life. I never imagined life could be this incredible and I want it for you, too. Will you join me?

What one choice will you now make, big or small, to move out of fear's slavery and into freedom? Write it down and commit to making it happen! Say "*yes*"—lift your chains and be free!

KIM CRUMPLER
Personal Style and Branding Coach,
Shopper and Speaker

(425) 503-9885
kim@uniquelysavvy.com
www.uniquelysavvy.com

From adverse beginnings to experiencing life in full bloom, Kim Crumpler is a style visionary who's discovered the magic of living her "authentic essence and style" and enthusiastically helps others achieve the same. Kim graduated from Central Washington University and founded Uniquely Savvy Inc. in 2000. She delivers customized style solutions to clients with diverse lifestyles and branding objectives both in Seattle and nationwide.

Kim passionately empowers individuals to step into their authentic essence and style from the inside-out and champions them in maximizing their potential. She inspires clients to discover and celebrate the strengths of their personal brand: skills, talents, abilities, personality and passions—the attributes that make an individual unique. Accurately translating that brand into a personal statement of style according to best practices for cut, color, lifestyle and budget is a reflection of Kim's attention to style detail.

A member of AICI, the Association of Image Consultants International, Kim is an inspiring speaker for a variety of audiences, including cruise line vacationers. Her 22 years of image and style experience provides reliable expertise for her Style GPS, Color Compass, Wow Factor wardrobe evaluation and personal shopping services.

Just Let Go

Risk-Taking Strategies for an Incredible Life

By Karen Roche, CDC

*H*ow many times in your life have you really wanted to achieve a goal or a dream? Or, how many times have you had a vision, a craving, a yearning to pursue something significant in your pursuit of happiness? All of these desires usually involve taking risks. Risk-taking is for passionate people who care about what they do and how they live on a daily basis. Risk-taking is for people who do not just daydream. Risk-taking is for people who are willing to do what it takes to create their incredible life.

Risk-taking is the act of doing something that scares you or makes you uncomfortable. Risk-taking is also when you do something you are not sure you will be successful at. The reason you take the risk is because you are in the pursuit of something bigger or better and your risk helps to get you there. When someone has a dream of running a marathon, a risk would be joining a running group even though they do not think they will be able to keep up with the more experienced athletes. Another example might be if someone has a desire to start their own business, even writing down their goal and telling someone who could help them could feel like a huge risk.

It is key to discuss risk-taking here in a book about how to have an incredible life because risk-taking is a key ingredient. Anything you pursue that you have never done before or have not been successful at before will involve some risk. It is your ability to take action in spite of your fear or discomfort in the pursuit of your goal or dream that will make your success that much sweeter and far more likely.

In this chapter, I will share with you the important things to know and do to become more of a risk-taker so that your incredible life comes to you faster and with more certainty.

A Feeling is Just a Feeling

As you get ready to take more risks and become more of a risk–taker, there are all kinds of feelings that you may be experiencing: trepidation, anxiety, even a little true fear. That is okay; know that all feelings are valid, they are part of what makes you the unique person you are. Listen to them, acknowledge them and recognize and realize that they are just feelings. Feelings change and pass. They do not have to stop you or sidetrack you. Once you take action in an area you were feeling anxious or uncomfortable about, you will find that the fear will dissipate—it actually goes away. Think about your first day at your first job: you were probably anxious, but that feeling dissipated significantly after the first day and was probably totally gone some days afterward. What do you want to do that you have not been doing because of the feelings that come up when you think about doing it? Maybe it is time to do it simply for the experience of watching the fearful feelings dissipate and watching the new, more positive feelings come in.

Put Yourself on a Mission

As you pursue your dreams and desires, you may encounter disappointments, digressions or naysayers. Make a decision right now to put yourself on a mission. Putting yourself on a mission means that you are committing yourself to your goal or dream and that you are going to see it through to completion even if it takes longer than you anticipated, even if you have setbacks, even if it calls you away from other things. What is it? Declare it, proclaim it. Is your mission to start a nonprofit, get to your ideal weight, build your dream home? It is only after you have put yourself on a mission that your risk-taking can begin.

Notice that I used the word *mission,* not *missions.* Too many missions or pursuits at once can overwhelm and exhaust you. One is enough for now. You decide what is right for you.

Quiet the Self-Defeating Voices

Have you reflected on a dream of a new career, new venture or new travel destination, only to be deflated by the voice inside of you that says, "No, don't do it!" "You are too old!" "You are too young!" "You don't have the time" or "You don't have the money"?

People stay in jobs they do not love because of the benefits and because they do not believe they could replace that income. People stay in unhealthy relationships because their partner pays the bills, and they do not think they could possibly survive on their own. If no risk or no action is taken, the self-defeating voices can continue until you feel overwhelmed, deflated and exhausted. This is when dreams and desires can slowly turn into fairy tales that soon fade away.

Know that the more you take risks, the less the self-defeating voices have to say, and the more your self-supporting voice wins your thoughts and gets your attention.

To quiet the self-defeating voices you hear, first recognize that thoughts are not the truth. Thoughts are just thoughts. They only have power when you give them power. When you notice a self-defeating thought, just let it fade and replace it with the thought you would like to be true. For example, perhaps you want to start a book club and the self-defeating thought comes in: "No one will want to get together with me and talk about books." Recognize the thought is self-defeating, dismiss it and replace it with a thought that represents what you want, such as: "There are people who will be thrilled to get together with me to discuss books."

Be more conscious of your thoughts. Which ones are serving you and which ones are preventing you from creating your incredible life? Replace those thoughts with self-supporting thoughts and you will find that the self-defeating thoughts will be greatly diminished.

> *"Action is the antidote to despair."*
> —Joan Baez, American folksinger

Step outside your comfort zone. Once you gain more control of your thinking, the next thing is to support that self-supportive thinking with self-supportive action.

Every time you do something you are apprehensive or anxious about or outright afraid to do, you are stepping out of your comfort zone and thereby expanding your comfort zone. Each time you do it, it is a cause for celebration. Every risk you take brings you closer to achieving your incredible life.

To get started stepping outside your comfort zone, first write down your goals. See Jan McDonough's chapter, *Goal Setting,* on page 21 for more detailed information. Then place your goals somewhere visible where you can read them two or three times a day. Next, pick a goal to work on and write down all the actions that will help you get there. Some of these actions will be scary or uncomfortable. Write them down anyway.

Do Something Risky Every Day

Sometimes when someone takes a risk they consciously or

unconsciously decide that they have done enough for awhile and the action stops. If you have something you want to create, do something every day to move you closer to that goal, dream or desire. For example, let's say that your goal is to become a hairdresser and open your own salon. Here are some daily actions to take to bring you closer to that goal.

Day 1: Call local cosmetology schools. Find out what the curriculum entails, what the hours are, financial obligations, etc. Make sure to write them down.

Day 2: Evaluate all of the different ways to acquire your education and decide on which one to complete. Commit to that decision.

Day 3: Sign up for the program, pay a deposit and make a financial commitment.

Day 4: Call area salons to see if there are any apprentice programs available. Get information on these programs.

Days 5-11: Each day, visit a salon and do an informational interview for the apprentice program.

Day 12: Decide which apprentice programs you want to be a part of and apply for your top three.

As you read this, you might think, "None of this seems very risky," and you might be right—for you. Recognize that for some people, talking to people about their future is scary; for others, going to places they have never been before makes them anxious. People often put off making decisions because making a decision is a commitment and means you have to do something about it.

Now let's talk about you. What is a goal or a dream you have that you have been putting off? Pick one. Then go ahead and write down your list of actions to take to get to your accomplishment. Now take the action for the first day and schedule the subsequent actions.

Taking Action Creates Positive Energy

Your risk-taking and actions will be rewarded in many ways, some you may anticipate and some you may not. One that you may not expect is the positive energy your action creates.

Once you commit to your dream to having true happiness, the energy of pursuing your dream will begin to stir up within your very core. Every action increases the energy of you moving toward your goal. Your whole life will be energized and full of more passion because you are taking risks and you are in action. There will come a time when you feel an openness, a freedom, an understanding that there are no more boundaries that hold you back from where you really need to be, and you will be right, because now you are a risk-taker.

Sometimes it will feel like magic. It is not magic. It is the positive energy you create around you when you commit and affirm your desire with every risk you take. It will make you more astute, more aware of anything or anyone who can support you or assist you in realizing your desire. Like when you run into someone you have been meaning to connect with for weeks or when something comes in the mail that is the perfect solution to a roadblock you expected to encounter. You can keep this energy and momentum present by staying in action and affirming your desires daily.

Pay Attention to Your Intuition

"Twenty years from now you will be more disappointed by the things that you didn't do than by the ones you did do. So throw off the bowlines. Sail away from the safe harbor. Catch the trade winds in your sails. Explore. Dream. Discover."
—Mark Twain, American writer and humorist

Risk-taking builds self-confidence and it also increases your self-knowing. You begin to see what is possible for you and what you are capable of. These benefits in turn can increase your intuition. With risk-taking and creating your incredible life, it is important to be tuned in to your intuition. Listen to what your gut tells you and what ideas, thoughts and feelings come from it.

I own a hair/fitness center and awhile back my business of six years was facing eviction after a series of unexpected expenses and mishaps with the landlord of the space we occupied. One day, I broke down and cried because I did not know what to do. I did not want to lose my business. I did not want to let down my longtime clients, many of whom were true friends. As I was just about to throw my hands up and quit, I walked by a vacant building I have walked by many times. As I passed the window, I got a feeling in my gut to make the call and see about the availability of the space. Long story short, within a week I had everything lined up to move in to this new location, the location that would soon triple my business.

By stepping back, taking a deep breath and listening to my intuition, I was able to strengthen myself and create a solution to a dire situation. Once you are in alignment with your purpose and in pursuit of your mission, you can heighten your awareness of your intuition and now add that ingredient to your recipe for creating what you want in your life.

Practice Patience, Persistence and Perseverance

"When you get in a tight place and everything goes against you, till it seems as though you could not hold on a minute longer, never give up then, for that is just the place and time that the tide will turn."
—Harriet Beecher Stowe, American abolitionist and author

Patience, persistence and perseverance are key in pursuing your incredible life and increasing your risk-taking. Sometimes our risks will give us instant results and sometimes they will not. It is okay to want results right away, but it will not always happen. You will have to be patient and persistent. If you do not see results quickly, do not give up. Do not be the person who says, "Well, at least I tried!" Don't try, do, as the wise Yoda said in the *Star Wars* movie, *The Empire Strikes Back.* For example, someone has a dream of being a songwriter. That person writes a song, enters a songwriting contest and does not win. He or she may have to enter several contests, take several classes, get an agent, do lots of things before realizing their dream. Persistence, perseverance and patience will be key ingredients in reaching your goal.

Where do you see that you are not being patient? Is there somewhere that you are not being persistent or persevering? Take a moment for reflection and write down your answers. Then decide if there are any actions or risks you want to take as a result of this exercise.

Go Ahead and Take That Risk!

We have discussed many things in this chapter that will support you in taking risks and creating your incredible life. You have probably had many thoughts and ideas for risks that would support you in your goals and dreams as you have read this chapter. Now it is time to get started. Be a risk-taker, be more of a risk-taker. Use risk-taking to accomplish your mission and create your incredible life. Begin today.

KAREN ROCHE, CDC
The KUR

Live your life to the fullest

(860) 232-0212
karen@theinnerkur.com
www.theinnerkur.com

Karen believes that life is to be lived to the fullest. After 23 years of being an entrepreneur in the field of hair and fitness, Karen has loved the journey of being able to be a part of her clients' lives. Her clients have taught her many valuable lessons about life, love and family, and have given her great wisdom to create her extraordinary life. Karen is a certified colorist and esthetician. Her expertise has led her to film projects, photo shoots, hair shows, educating and much more. Her goal is to help you look your best and to feel confident about being you.

Karen established a beautiful fitness and health studio, "The KUR" (which stands for "Know Who You Are), dedicated to helping people become healthy physically, mentally and spiritually. Karen is also the proud mother of four beautiful children whom she adores. In 2009 she became a Certified Dream Coach.® Karen has always lived life with passion and purpose. She is a firm believer that you can achieve your dreams with perseverance and passion. Karen teaches others how to achieve their dreams and goals.

Life is to be lived! Enjoy!

Give a Little—Get a Lot
Service to the Community as a Rich Life Strategy
By Michele Rastovich, CDC

"Living is the art of loving. Loving is the art of caring.
Caring is the art of sharing. Sharing is the art of living.
If you want to lift yourself up, lift up someone else."
—Booker T. Washington, American educator,
author and civil rights leader

*L*ooking to add more energy, passion, or richness to your life? Add a little service to the community. You might be asking how you could possibly add one more thing to your "to do" list, especially something like volunteer work, with no monetary reward. Or you might be thinking, "Sure, I'd like to do something—as soon as I retire, or as soon as the kids are grown, or as soon as my bills are paid." Why wait? Volunteering is a powerful tool in not only making the world a better place, but also in helping you live the life of your dreams. Doing something for someone else is a key strategy for living a fulfilled, richer life. Giving, sharing, helping and caring for others gives you more feelings of fulfillment and purpose than the best car, the fanciest pair of shoes or the most decadent day at the spa ever could.

The work provided by volunteers reduces the burden on public and private spending and uplifts the lives of those who have great need. As nonprofit services—organizations supporting the environment, the arts, community health and public schools across the country—lose funding, it has never been more important for each of us to consider how even small actions make a big difference. Organizations rely on volunteers to continue their work. Volunteer contributions are essential to our society and contribute to the overall well-being of our communities.

But volunteering is more than just giving. It is an exchange. It provides as much benefit, or more, to the volunteer as it does for the cause, organization or individual receiving the volunteer's time. Have you ever seen the look on a volunteer's face when he or she hands a toy to a child and see her beaming from this generous gesture? Usually the volunteer's smile is as big and radiant as the child's. The benefits of volunteering are as diverse as volunteers themselves. Just a few reasons volunteers give for being involved in service to their communities include: gaining a sense of purpose, feeling pride in contribution, making new friends, gaining skills and experience, building self-esteem, feeling needed and important, connecting with others, exploring new career and hobby options, using creative gifts, fighting boredom, loneliness and depression, and having fun. Typical benefits can be grouped into three integral elements for living the life of your dreams: increased life satisfaction; improved wellness; and unlimited possibility.

Service to the Community Increases Life Satisfaction

If you have lost touch with what truly gives you joy, volunteering offers the chance to explore your interests. True happiness comes when you do what you are most passionate about. Think of a time when you lost all sense of time. Chances are, you were doing something you truly loved and were using your natural gifts. When you identify your passions, you can find volunteer opportunities that will let you give to others while doing what you love.

A sense of accomplishment is also an important element of life satisfaction. Doing good things for others or the community increases your sense of personal achievement. In my twenty years of experience working with volunteers, I have heard them say many times that the satisfaction of helping others, and of being part of a larger community, gives them a more positive view of their life and their future. In successfully taking on new challenges in your volunteer work, you become more aware of your capabilities. The more you know about your own gifts and skills, the greater your self-confidence; and the greater your self-confidence, the more power you have to change your life.

Virtually every framework for self-development tells us that if we want a more fulfilled life, being thankful for what we already have is key. Volunteering helps us recognize our many blessings and provides an opportunity to express that gratitude through service. People with rich life experiences have broader views of their local communities and of the global community. The broader your world view, the better problem solver and creative thinker you are. Volunteering exposes you to different cultures, different faiths, different values and different ways of doing business. You learn to appreciate, and work with, people's differences.

Service to the Community Promotes Good Health

You have probably heard it before—do something for someone else and you will feel better. Now science has proven it in a growing body of research. In 2007, the Corporation for National and Community Service, Office of Research and Policy Development, published *The Health Benefits of Volunteering: A Review of Recent Research,* which stated that people who volunteer have better physical, mental and emotional health than those who do not. Volunteers have greater longevity, fewer symptoms of chronic pain and heart disease, and a stronger immune system.

Another key component of wellness is being part of a larger community. Belonging or being a part of a community is a concept humanity has recognized going all the way back to Abraham Maslow's Hierarchy of Needs, first introduced in 1943 in his paper, "A Theory of Human Motivation," published in *The Psychological Review*.

Regular contact with others protects against stress and depression. During a particularly difficult time in Lynn's life, she managed to force herself out of the house one night to volunteer at a local continuing education program for adults. Although it would have been easier to stay home, she returned the following week. Even doing simple tasks like filing helped change her perspective for a few hours, and she saw that what she was doing was a huge help to the program. By the third week, she could not wait to go back. Meeting new people, concentrating on something other than her problems, even for a short time, and being part of something bigger than herself, lifted her spirits and reduced her sense of anxiety.

Whether you think of your community as your neighborhood, a geographic location or simply the community of people who share your interests and values, connecting to them in meaningful ways will improve your overall health. When we see ourselves as engaged in important work that makes a difference to others, our psychological well-being improves.

Volunteering also keeps our brains young. In challenging ourselves to be intellectually and socially engaged, our brains stay sharper. Memory is improved and functionality is preserved.

Service to the Community Opens Up Possibilities

Volunteering can put you in contact with influential people from all walks of life and professions, which builds your social and professional network. When you expand your network, you learn about new resources and new opportunities and create space for new ideas. When his city councilwoman came to speak to his class, Derek thought he was just in for another boring lecture. He complained about a local issue, and the councilwoman challenged him to work with her. Together they developed a citywide art project where young people learned about the cost of illegal graffiti to the community, artists were provided a venue for their work, community members worked across generations and local businesses got involved. As a result of his community involvement, Derek met an adult mentor who has advised him, been a role model for him and has shown him many possibilities for himself. He also has a huge sense of pride for uplifting others in his community—all because he agreed to help.

Volunteer jobs also provide on-the-job training experience. According to the February 2009 *Career Xroads® 8th Annual Source of Hire Study,* by Gerry Crispin and Mark Mehler, up to 60 percent of job vacancies are filled internally or through external networking, with little or no public advertising. Whether you are entering or re-entering the workforce, considering a career change, want to learn new skills or practice existing skills, volunteering can help you try different kinds of work in a safe learning environment. It allows you to try new things without making a long-term commitment. In trying new tasks, meeting new people and assuming new responsibilities, you may discover natural gifts and talents you did not know you had.

Volunteering is also fun! Volunteers choose their jobs carefully and are appreciated for their contributions. They are doing something for the love of it, and that is just pure fun. When we are having fun, we are able to see new possibilities we never imagined.

Volunteering—Six Simple Ideas to Get You Started

Volunteer opportunities are limited only by your imagination. Whether you want to beef up your résumé, have new experiences, discover your passion or change the world one person at a time, there is a volunteer project with your name on it. By spending a little bit of time considering what you really want in your life, you can find a volunteer opportunity that meets your needs and supports your dreams. Consider what you want to add to your life and do a little research. Build a house in your community or dig wells in South America. Monitor kittens at your local animal shelter or white lions in South Africa. Coach a local youth sports team or work with orphans in India. Start where you are now, be open to new possibilities, and see how far you can go.

Is your dream to have more time for the arts and entertainment? Many entertainment venues depend on volunteers from the community to help run things. Look for an opportunity that matches your interests. As a volunteer usher, see shows you love. Volunteer at a music festival and meet people who love music. Volunteer with a community theater and use your creative talents to help with everything from ticket sales to costumes. Carol gets to see as many summer concerts as she wants in exchange for volunteering a couple of hours a month as a guide, showing tourists around and answering questions. Take advantage of the Web and Internet search engines. Put in the name of your community along with words like "volunteer" or "arts" and see what pops up.

Is your dream to travel? Combine what you love to do with travel to the places you want to see. Consider teaching what you know, building houses, working on an organic farm. Volunteer opportunities in another community or even another country are easy to research on the Internet. More and more nonprofit organizations are catering to travelers looking for volunteer vacations. Opportunities can require few skills, like cleanup work, or highly sophisticated skills like providing medical services, and everything in between. Commitments could range from a day or two to six months or more.

Volunteer vacationers are diverse, but typically share a desire to do something good while also experiencing new places and challenges in locales they might not otherwise visit. Bonnie visits Mexico once a year. By combining her mission work with her vacation, she is able to see parts of the Mexican culture most tourists never see. Check out the amazing volunteer travel possibilities at www.i-to-i.com, www.globalcitizens.org, or www.lonelyplanet.com/volunteer.

Is your dream to work on the environment? There are also volunteer vacations that engage people in scientific research and education to promote the sustainability of our global community. Although volunteers often pay a fee to cover some expenses, they can travel as far as the Amazon or the Arctic. If working on the environment is your thing, you can also make a difference close to home. Becci combines her love of the beach by leading lectures for local beachcombers and, as a Master Gardener, Kathy teaches her neighbors how to garden without pesticides. For international opportunities, see www.earthworks.org. For national opportunities, visit www.sierraclub.org or search on the Web for the name of your community and "environment" and see where it leads.

Is your dream to share your expertise? What ever your talents, hobbies or passions, somebody else wants to learn about them or could benefit from them. Assess your skills and think about where they might be useful. Love language? Consider teaching English to new immigrants, or creative writing to teens. Have a green thumb? Share your love of gardening with a local park or city department. Are you an expert on local history? How about volunteering at the local museum, or leading walking tours of your city. Ramona shares her love of horses by being a 4-H Club Leader. As she teaches third, fourth and fifth graders about horsemanship, they learn belonging, mastery, generosity and independence. For international work, browse www.i-to-i.com. To share your knowledge locally, start with your local

United Way office, schools, special interest clubs or youth organizations.

Is your dream to fix a problem in your community? Next time you think, "Somebody should fix that," remember you are Somebody. Ask yourself what you want to accomplish—who do you want to help and how? Is there a way to accomplish your goal by volunteering with an existing organization, or will it take a larger effort to make a difference? Perhaps starting your own nonprofit is the best answer. When Sarri was tired of seeing her students "couch surfing," or worse, sleeping outside, because they did not have homes to go to, she discovered her dream. It was not easy. But by enrolling others in her dream, she navigated a complex bureaucratic system to start Cocoon House, a nonprofit providing emergency and transitional housing for teens.

Is your dream to try new things, then be done? Volunteering can be short-term or long-term. If you are not keen on long-term commitments, consider how to use your skills and interests for a once-only or once-a-year project. Love to organize? Start a food drive or blood drive in your work place. Love to entertain? Donate a gourmet dinner as a fund raiser. Love to connect people? Plan a project for people from different parts of your community. When Bobi heard an interesting idea, she invited others to help plan an event to connect community members with local charities. In addition to the many new partnerships and friendships that were formed, the Alternative Gift Fair raised over $20,000 in just four hours.

More Volunteering Ideas

IS YOUR DREAM TO:	HOW ABOUT:
Make a difference in the life of just one person?	Mentoring a child, being a lunch buddy for a student, or serving at a Senior Center.

IS YOUR DREAM TO:	HOW ABOUT:
Be more active or physically fit?	Rebuilding a nature trail, maintaining a public park, rehabilitating a stream, coaching a youth team or teaching an exercise class.
Meet new people?	Joining a group that shares your interests. Do more than just attend meetings. Volunteer to work on a project.
Live a simpler, clutter-free life?	Organizing your friends and neighbors to clean out closets. Your clutter could be a gold mine for organizations that provide clothes and household items.

Before you commit. Volunteer opportunities that match your goals and interests will be most fulfilling. With a little bit of homework, you will ensure that while giving to the community, you are also gaining what you want. Ask yourself the following questions:

- **What do you want to gain?** Do you want to learn something new or explore new interests? Or do you want to spend more time doing what you already know or love? Do you want to meet new people, live healthier, have more fun or simply make a difference?

- **What kind of work do you want to do?** Do you want to organize an event, or work directly with people in need? Do you like being behind the scenes, or up front? Do you want to work with a big organization or a small grass roots group? Do you want to be inside or outside? Do you want to be physically active or work at a desk? Do you want a flexible schedule with a lot of different tasks, or do you prefer more structure?

- **What do you feel most strongly about?** What are the issues closest to your heart? Are they around social justice issues? Basic needs?

Public policy? Issues affecting children? Youth? Families? The environment? If you only have so much time to share, what are your priority issues?

- **How much time can you commit?** Be realistic. Over-committing can make your volunteer job seem too burdensome and just one more commitment you resent. Are you looking for a long-term or short-term commitment? Do you have a couple of hours a week or several days a month that you can dedicate? Even an hour or two a month can have a huge impact on the organization, and on you.

- **What will the organization expect of you?** Interview the agency to make sure you want to volunteer for them. Ask specific questions about the position. Be clear about your role and your tasks. What exactly will you be doing? How much time will the position require? What skills will you be able to use and develop? Who will you be working with? Who will you answer to?

"I don't know what your destiny will be, but one thing I do know: the only ones among you who will be really happy are those who have sought and found how to serve."
—Albert Schweitzer,
Alsatian German-French philosopher and physician

The best volunteer experiences are win-win situations. Your generosity can change the world. Demonstrating your own spirit through service to the community will be as transformational for you as it is for those who receive your generosity. Volunteering will give your heart, body and soul a boost. You will be happier and healthier, have a purpose, and a great sense of self satisfaction. Integrating what you love, what you want to learn and what you want more of in your life with service to others for as little as two hours a week will bring huge benefits. Do what you can because you can. See what needs to be done and do it—your own way. Your rewards will be many.

MICHELE RASTOVICH, CDC
Bring Your Best Self

(425) 339-6059
michele@bringyourbestself.com
www.bringyourbestself.com

Michele always loved hearing stories. Today, she uses that love to help people listen to the stories of their own lives to rediscover their passion. As a Certified Dream Coach,® she uses proven strategies to guide clients in remembering what gives them joy, envisioning the life of their dreams, and developing solid action plans to live it every day. She is a lively and energetic speaker, a member of the training team for the highly acclaimed *Art and Science of Community Organizing* and a presenter for the powerful *Create Your Future Now*® workshops.

As a skilled facilitator, Michele also works with community organizations to help them discover the stories they want to create. Living "in community" is a cornerstone of Michele's life. If you asked her who her people are, she would answer people who see possibilities, people who find joy in everyday experience and people who use their gifts to be of service. She brings more than twenty years experience in community organizing—promoting collaboration, communication, commitment and cultural competency—to advocate for programs and public policies that support children and families.

Circle of Your Dreams
Getting Back on Track after Difficult Times
By Daria Vallentiny

*"In times of profound change, the learners inherit the earth, while
the learned find themselves beautifully equipped to deal
with a world that no longer exists."*
—Al Rogers, co-founder of Global Schoolnet

*I*n the modern, tumultuous world in which we live, change comes at a rapid and relentless speed. We need resiliency to live well. Resiliency refers to your ability to quickly recover from change, misfortune or setbacks, enabling you to lead a healthy and fulfilling life. The key to resilience and to your ability to recover from setbacks is your connection to the circle of your dreams. The circle of your dreams comprises your passions. It is your reason for living.

Painful feelings often surface when you feel "trapped" and without choices. During extreme and traumatic life-altering changes, you sometimes lose your sense of security. As important parts of your world that you once knew cease to exist, you struggle to adjust accordingly. In order to triumph over life circumstances that you cannot change, you must learn to let go of the past and embrace new experiences. You were born with the ability to move your life forward into your next phase of life, for life is a journey of constant change.

My life as a mother, as a business professional and as a woman was drastically affected by my life-altering experience. My 33-year-old daughter, Cydni, died unexpectedly in 2006 from an aortic aneurysm two weeks after giving birth to her fourth child. While struggling to adjust to my loss, I also had to adjust to many other changes—becoming a guardian for two of my four grandchildren, caring for my aging mother, and a major organizational change at my job of twenty years. I temporarily lost my purpose and passion for life. I became numb and operated on autopilot, barely managing to get through each day. Nevertheless, by choosing the path of gratitude over the path of grief, I moved out of a ring of fire into the circle of my dreams. I was able to be reborn with a new direction in life. I now dedicate a part of my life to helping others cross over and recover from their traumatic life experiences.

Change is a certainty in life. It is necessary if you are going to grow. This chapter will address techniques you can use to recover from life-altering experiences. You will learn how to:

- Overcome the ring of fire that prevents you from fully enjoying your life while adjusting to change.

- Connect to the circle of your dreams, the passion within you, in order to extinguish any ring of fire that surrounds you.

- Bounce back with a new strength to resume your direction in life or to create a new direction.

The Ring of Fire

"I've lived to bury my desires and see my dreams corrode with rust.
Now all that's left are fruitless fires that burn
my empty heart to dust."
—Alexander Sergeivich Pushkin, Russian author

Small changes and challenges occur daily. They drain away some of your energy reserves. Bigger changes drain even more. A rapid series of changes or a traumatic event can deplete your entire energy reserve. When your energy resources are depleted, you have no energy left for life. You may experience "burnout" or fall into a depression. There is a lack of motivation. You may experience hopelessness and aloneness. Life seems dreary.

The ring of fire comprises your fears, losses, doubts, hatred, anger and pain. The flames consume all of your energy, leaving you with a very low reserve to cope with day-to-day living. The restricting smoke from the fire is suffocating. It limits your ability to focus on your life and clouds your view of the world outside. You are surrounded by hopelessness with no vision of your path in life. There is no recovery in sight.

Many smart and talented people suffer from setbacks in life triggered by events such as job loss, the death of a loved one, becoming a caretaker for a terminally ill family member, recovery from a debilitating illness, surviving breast cancer or being a victim of domestic violence or sexual assault. They lose their zeal and zest for life. These events impact their personal, professional and spiritual relationships and their ability to perform in their roles as parent, spouse, corporate leader or entrepreneur. When you lose sight of your dreams and goals, you stop living your life. You become surrounded by the ring of fire by giving more attention to your fears and doubts instead of focusing on your happiness or quality of life. Fortunately, you were born with the ability to handle traumatic experiences.

Overcoming the Ring of Fire

"Too many of us are not living our dreams
because we are living our fears."
—Les Brown, American motivational speaker, author

You cannot survive the burning rage of the ring of fire. You can, however, extinguish the flames and step outside the ring. Just as when you survive a trauma, you cannot change what has happened, but you can control your reaction to it. Here are some tips on how to survive traumatic events in order to move on with your life.

Take time to heal. Your experiences and your feelings are unique and personal. Your road to recovery and healing after a life-altering experience is also unique and personal. Your return to normalcy is at your own individual pace. Don't rush through the process of recovery. Faster is not always better in all situations—like making love, eating or building a relationship. It will take as long as it takes for you to heal. There will sometimes be setbacks along the way. Allow yourself the time you need. Be compassionate and patient with yourself if things are moving more slowly than you would like.

Acknowledge your pain. Have you ever been lost on a road trip trying to get from point A to point B? Once you realize that you are lost, you can do something to get yourself back on course. You can use your GPS, consult a map, ask someone for directions or go back to the place where you were certain that you were on the right road. This is also true in life when dealing with life-altering situations. Admit to your fears, your loss, your anger, your doubts and your pain. Once you acknowledge it, you can take actions to get your life back on track and the healing process can begin. Let go of blame. Let go of anger. Let go of all the feelings that feed the ring of fire. You need to focus your energy on getting through the experience. Channeling your energy to healing starts with extinguishing the ring of fire and accepting your new circumstance.

Plot your new course. Being lost on a road trip can be very frustrating. You find relief once you get back on track and move toward your destination. This is true with the healing process, too. The ring of fire is diminished even more once you plan your recovery course. The key to recovery is connecting to your circle of dreams. Sylvia Boorstein, a Jewish grandmother, psychotherapist and Buddhist wrote, "We can struggle, or we can surrender." Surrender means wisely accommodating ourselves to what is beyond our control. By plotting a new course, we accept the change, adjust our attitude and move on with our life. Is there a new course you want to plot? Are there any dreams to which you would like to reconnect? We will explore that next.

The Circle of Dreams

"As life progresses and we continue to transform and refine our consciousness, we gain more insight and humility, greater strength of character, and deeper faith in the meaningfulness of life."
—Elizabeth Lesser, author and co-founder of Omega Institute

The circle of dreams comprises all that makes you happy. It could be what makes you smile, a beautiful sunset, a favorite song, a visit from a friend or a good massage. Your passions fuel the core of the circle. By engaging in activities to strengthen the core of the circle, you will defuse the hold that any traumatic events have over you. By choosing to engage in activities that strengthen you, you will eventually let go of your fears, doubts, hurt and despair.

There is an age-old question: "What comes first, the chicken or the egg?" To embark on the path of change, you will need motivation and action. Fortunately, it does not matter which comes first. You can take actions that will cause you to be motivated or you can be motivated to take action. Remember that your new motto will become: "One day at a time." As you become more purposeful, your mind will start working again. You will find yourself seeking realistic solutions to problems posed by the new change. You will eventually get to a thirty-day plan, but you need to start initially with daily activities to build your strength and to help you regain your energy, clarity and focus. This will help you to see the circle of your dreams from the ring of fire in order to cross over.

> *"First say to yourself what you would be;*
> *and then do what you have to do."*
> —Epictetus, Greek philosopher

The circle begins with you. At this point in life, you may be so lost that you have no idea who you are. You identify yourself by your possessions, your status in life, your appearance, your job or your relationships. When one of these areas is impacted negatively, you become confused regarding your value. Take time to define who you are, your goals and your purpose in life. Don't confuse what you have with who you are. Below are three questions the late Dr. James Scott Kennedy, noted playwright and professor, told his children to ask themselves each day. These questions are a good daily ritual for you to incorporate to ensure you are connected to your purpose and following your path in life.

• "Who am I?" This question refers to who you are at your core.

• "Where am I?" Where are you on your path in life?

• "What must I do to be me?" How can you lead a life based on authenticity?

Take time to reflect. During your recovery, learn to savor moments of happiness that happen to you. Make a list at the end of each day of the good things that have happened—a song you heard, a good meal, good weather, a smile from a stranger, receiving a call or email from a good friend. Daily journaling can help you to connect to your inner guide and help you to express your hidden deep feelings.

Make sure that a portion of your daily journaling or reflection time includes your list of gratitude. Being grateful is an important part of your healing process. You need to be aware of your gifts and strengths in your present life. The most important meeting of any day is the meeting you have with yourself.

Link to a support group. If you are fortunate, family and friends will gather around you initially to show you love and support during your time of change and struggle. But their support may taper before you completely heal and your energy reserves are replenished. You may be left alone to continue your fight to regain control of your new life. Although it may be hard to let go of the past that you had, over time, your old life will lose its controlling power as you embrace the next engaging chapter of your life. During the transition, seek a support group you can join. Join an Internet group or start a blog to continue to express your anger as well as your need to heal. Find a therapist for group or individual therapy or a life coach for added support. Your situation will be understood better by those battling to recover from their own similar, yet unique, struggles. It is important that you be able to express your feelings in order to heal. Remember that your negative thoughts and feelings are part of what fuels the ring of fire.

Fuel the circle of dreams. Devote each day to one activity that fuels the circle of your dreams. Choose at least one item from the list on the next page, depending on your preferences and time, or add your own favorite activities. Sometimes it helps to add activities that you have never done, always wanted to do or never made time to do. You may have to force yourself to do this but the end result will be invaluable. Remember, you don't need motivation to take action. And, if it helps, invite a friend to join you and hold you accountable.

CIRCLE OF DREAMS ACTIVITY CHART		
Listen to music	Volunteer	Go dancing
Get a massage	Buy a new book	Go the movies
Read a book	Go to church	Go out to a restaurant
Talk with a friend	Pray	Learn yoga
Go for a walk	Meditate	Learn to knit or sew
Watch the sunset or rise	Exercise	Take a ceramics class
Look at the stars	Join a gym	Take a dance class
Spend time gardening	Make your favorite meal	Go for a swim
Learn to fly a plane	Plan a vacation	Take a train trip
Join a book club	Play a sport	Go on a cruise
Play the piano	Take up photography	Learn a foreign language
Go to a museum	Go on a hike	Take a bubble bath
Do a puzzle	Paint a picture	Train for a marathon

The Path of Gratitude

"We are moving toward a New World...a world where POWER is not defined by how much control you have over others, but how much control you have over your Self."
—Teresa Kay-Aba Kennedy,
American health and productivity management expert

Each of us writes our own history of sorrow and gladness. Some people learn and grow from their misfortunes in life while others become more bitter, more reactive and more cynical. Your recovery from adversity is characterized by the paths that you choose for healing your spirit and moving forward. It is characterized by the control you exert over yourself. Choose the path of gratitude over the path of grief and regret. It will lead you to the circle of your dreams.

Life is a journey. It is full of change. Success in this new era depends on your resiliency—your ability to be innovative, creative and resourceful in solving problems for which there may have been no precedents. Stay connected to who you are and who you are meant to become by keeping your energies and spirit high. You will find new energy and maintain control over your life by connecting to your purpose and passion.

You were born to fly.
Spread your wings and soar.
Remember to connect to the circle of your dreams
wherein lies the passion within you
that is strong enough to put out any ring of fire
that dares to surround you.

DARIA VALLENTINY
Results Coaching Alliance

Dream it, Believe it, Achieve it!

(510) 543-6774
daria@resultscoachingalliance.com
www.resultscoachingalliance.com

Daria is the co-founder and owner of Results Coaching Alliance. She and her business partner reside in Northern California and offer services to individuals and corporate clients nationwide. They have developed a proven system to help their clients produce the results they want in order to move their personal and professional goals forward. Daria is an innovative thinker and a visionary leader, an award–winning and inspiring speaker, workshop facilitator, author, certified life coach and small business consultant.

Daria encourages her clients and audiences with her inspiring messages, which are both provocative and encouraging. As a six-time marathon finisher, she gets her clients to cross the finish line one step at a time. They learn to believe in themselves and to have the courage to become the extraordinary person that they were born to be. She shares with them the healing powers found along the path of gratitude and appreciation as they heal and reconnect to their inner strengths. Her gentle, nurturing style and passion for guiding others through challenging times enables her to help her clients learn new methods to achieve results.

Wow! And This Too is a Perfect Moment
Taking Accountability for the Direction of Your Life
By Teena Tautkus, CDC

"The dream was always running ahead of me. To catch up, to live for a moment in unison with it, that was the miracle."
—Anaïs Nin, French modernist writer

Perfect Moments

As I gaze from the earth upward to the dark, predawn sky, the old tree bordering my sloping driveway in the front yard speaks volumes about life. Its aged branches extend outward, opening itself to all possibility. As it takes my eyes up, there is a brilliant silver moon dancing amongst glistening stars. I am joyous that I stopped to absorb this miraculous scene—the grandeur of a welcoming winter sky. This was a perfect moment.

As you create your own perfect moment, be silent. Look at everything, everywhere. Keep your head held nobly. Expand your lungs, taking in air through your nostrils. Feel your body relax, resigning, allowing you to capture what has always been there to see. Savor every sampling and consume as much as possible as often as you can.

Purposeful Moments

When I told my dad I was writing a chapter for a book entitled

Incredible Life, he said, "You can definitely write a book (meaning I have had enough life experiences), but you haven't had an incredible life." Incredible means unbelievable, seeming too unusual or improbable to be possible, unimaginable. That was his perception and I accepted that. There may have been some of you who reacted and thought, how could he say such a thing?

I have come to learn that *every* experience in life is on purpose, that the vast majority of the human race intends to be loving and kind, not mean and hurtful. As I paused, I felt in my dad's words love and sorrow simultaneously flooding him with raw emotion. There were occurrences in my life that he could not have spared me from. I knew that he was reliving, for as brief a moment as it was, those experiences in the teleprompter of his mind. To him, my miscarriage, my shocking divorce and breakup of my family and how hard he saw I had to work to "do it all," were beyond his thinking and broke his heart. Purposefully and with my chest rising, I simply responded to him with a quietness and peace I knew came from deep within my soul, "Dad, I have an incredible life." This was a purposeful moment.

If Dad had not said what he did, I may not have viewed a quick snapshot of my life and come to the conclusion that indeed I have an incredible life. We each have our own list of hardships sandwiched between beautiful moments that far outweigh the not-so-good ones. There will always be speed bumps along the road of life to slow us down—our caution that we are traveling too fast. Do we have our own clear perception or do we let others cloud our view?

Take your time navigating over the obstacles, listening carefully to the sweet stillness of your yearning heart. You will hear magnificent, angelic sounds. When we stop to adjust the dial, clear the frequency and static of our doubting thoughts, we will be tuned in. Accelerate your senses—seeing, hearing, smelling, tasting and feeling. These are tools to discovering and enjoying your own purposeful moments.

Humorous Moments

When was the last time you lightened up and laughed? Are you too serious all the time? Recently I traveled to Corte Madera, California, for an Inspiring Speaker Training. My flight departed from Bradley International Airport in Windsor Locks, Connecticut, at 6 p.m. EST, with a connecting flight in Atlanta, Georgia, then on to San Francisco, California. Since I live on the East Coast, there would be a three-hour time difference when reaching my final destination. The departing flight from Atlanta was delayed two hours due to severe rain showers and damaging winds on the West Coast. My original midnight arrival into San Francisco was now 2 a.m. PST.

Eagerly, in hopes of getting a little sleep, I made my way off the crowded plane. I rapidly claimed my luggage, swiftly navigated the numerous travelers and took my curbside stance where I knew the Marin Transporter would whisk me out to Corte Madera. I waited for a bit, only to get the intuitive guidance that it was probable the Marin Transporter had ceased operating for the night. That was confirmed with a cell phone call and no answer from their office. Looking at the line of anxiously waiting, aggressively honking cabs in front of me, I inquired of a driver his ability to take me where I needed to go and the fare for such a journey. Arriving at the America's Best Value Inn at 3 a.m., we unloaded my luggage, I paid the fare and hesitantly I let the driver depart. What could go wrong?

I proceeded toward the front desk only to pull on the door and find it was locked. Noticing a doorbell, I pressed it; no response. I dialed the front desk and was relieved when a tall, groggy, dark-haired young man appeared from the back. He asked if he could help me, I responded that I was checking in. We went through the normal check-in procedure.

He handed me the key card and advised me my room was 117. I made my way to my room, swiped the card in the right-side slot. No click, no green light entry. Changing hands, I then swiped the card in the left-side slot. No click, no green light entry. I flipped the card over to read the directions—yes, I know you are supposed to do that first—to find there was no magical formula for scanning this card. I once again swiped on the right-side slot. Still no click, still no green light entry, but much to my wide-eyed amazement, the door opened and there, standing before me, was a man in only his boxer briefs. We made eye contact, he said nothing and I creatively replied, "Sorry, they told me this was my room. I guess that is why they call it the Best Value Inn, they assign you a roommate."

I chuckled, he gave me a bewildered smile, closed the door and I had a fit of laughter en route to the front desk. Composing myself, I phoned the attendant, reminding him who I was. I explained someone was already in room 117; there was silence. Finally he responded, "You are in room 115." This was a humorous moment.

You have to be able to laugh at your imperfections. As you continue to read more, I want you to envision that inside *every* single moment of your life are multiple moments to laugh about, be aware of and make into moments that will be forever imprinted on your heart and soul. Do you live your life to its fullest? What moments have you captured, like a young child catches a firefly in a jar, to explore, observe, and then set free? Remember the excitement as you ran into the house to show your family what you had caught. Have that same childlike enthusiasm about sharing your dreams, intentions and discoveries, no matter how young or mature you may be. This is when you learn about yourself and become clear about what matters to you. It is when we share with others, first those we trust the most to rally with us, that you take accountability for the direction of your life.

*"The human race has one really effective weapon,
and that is laughter."*
—Mark Twain, American author and humorist

Character Moments

Steve, 52, my boss, mentor and friend, left this world too soon for those of us he left behind. His independent spirit gave him a belief there were no limitations—those were only what we put on ourselves. I wondered as I sat through the memorial service what legacy I may leave behind. For, in his short lifetime, there were incredible and simple accomplishments. How would your eulogy read? When I think of Steve, I visualize the flight of the eagle. Strong, with its wings spread to their full expanse, it would soar uninhibited through the air, an illumination of spirit, healing and creation. His independent compass soared everyday of his life.

Steve charted the course of his life with every choice and direction he took. When talking to my friend and life coach, Althea, I explained that I believed our lives were predestined, but she said, "We still get to make our own choices." And, based on a choice, our life can unexpectedly be rewritten. No one knows what stirs you within like you do. Use your internal compass to guide you every day. What lies before you are experiences, discoveries—a new world to make yours. Delight in every sampling and devour as much as possible repeatedly. People who live their lives being the person they were born to be are happier, healthier and more fulfilled. What person are you going to be? What do you want? Are you living in integrity?

Transformational Moments

Victoria's journey to shed over 100 pounds was not just about the weight she chose to abandon. It was about being vulnerable, exposed, peeling back the layers of her life to acceptance of herself in her perfectly imperfect body. She shared that her father relentlessly criticized her—no matter how hard she tried, she still could not please him. Instead, it was about her pleasing herself. It is hard not to care what others think; it takes extra strength to stand tall and believe in yourself.

When we were infants learning to walk, our parents did not just let go and push us along our way and expect us to walk without falling. Instead, they guided us, helping us to balance and move forward one step at a time, until we built up the confidence, strength and practice to do it on our own. We can apply that same technique today, by simply not being afraid to *ask* for what we want. Generally speaking, people want to be needed. If you ask, the probability is high that the person you asked would be there for you. As I said, you simply need to do it. Seeing you succeed makes them feel a sense of accomplishment, too.

I was fortunate to work with Emily, who felt lost when her relationship had ended, leaving her with a disempowered, empty feeling. She was not certain she had the strength to handle this disappointment. When we got together, we talked about a plan of action for defining expectations, redirecting her anxious feelings by journaling—a strong suit for her—and being creative. We took what felt to her like negative traits and made them positive. You see, how you personally process is critical. It has to be customized to you as an individual— what works for one may not work for another. During our time together, she was provided tools, but it was her ultimate decision to make the change necessary to make a difference in achieving the life she talked about having. Months had passed since I had last seen her when our paths crossed again. We hugged one another, she looked incredible, and the confidence she exuded and the brilliance of her smile showed me she had found her own true direction. It is during the storms in our lives that we learn to navigate our way.

We remember and hear prolonged negative words and feelings, which can replay over and over again in our minds. During these hard realizations, we may not believe in ourselves. Each of you, through your own remarkable life journeys, can courageously unveil amazing men and women of strength, beauty and wisdom. Sometimes you have to find someone else who believes in you first, before you believe in yourself. These were transformational moments.

*"I like being tested. I get as scared as anyone.
But the feeling of putting yourself on the line, putting
your talent out there, betting on yourself and having it work,
is the most exhilarating feeling in the world."*
—Conan O'Brien, American comic and television show host

Reflective Moments

The *American Heritage Dictionary* defines "reflect" as *to give back or show an image; mirror.* You have your own book of life experiences that present you with your incredible life. Be aware of the image reflected back at you. Take five minutes every day, look in a mirror—it can be the rearview mirror of your car—and tell yourself, "I love you" and "you are a beautiful person." You will begin to believe this reality. You are the eagle spreading its wings, soaring higher, allowing yourself to capture your full potential. Seize *every* moment. They are gifts to take any time you desire. Heighten your senses—seeing, hearing, smelling, tasting and feeling—and find pleasure in your own reflective moment.

*"Aerodynamically, the bumble bee shouldn't be able to fly, but the
bumble bee doesn't know it so it goes on flying anyway."*
—Mary Kay Ash, Founder of Mary Kay, Inc.

Another Perfect Moment

As I purposely fix my eyes on that old tree bordering my sloping driveway, miniature volumes of my life have witnessed themselves to me. My aged recollections, like its branches, have allowed me to extend outward, opening myself to all possibility. My roving eyes move upward to the dazzling full moon gleaming amongst dull stars in a gray predawn sky. The scene is exceptional—the grandeur of a new winter sky anticipating the adventures of a new year. As of this moment, as I conclude this chapter, I have had 1,608,336,000 moments to make a difference, to weave into the fabric of my life. What colors are woven into yours?

As you create your own perfect moment, be hushed. Look far and wide, in all places. Keep your head held graciously. Inflate your lungs, feeling the sensation the new air gifts you. Your body will unwind, calm down, and lighten up to capture what is always there to see. Savor every sampling and consume as much as possible as often as you can, for in all moments are a gift of self. Life's moments are to be experienced with openness and unconditional love, and no matter what course you have traveled, it was the exact one for you.

TEENA TAUTKUS, CDC
Speaker, Trainer

(860) 306-7876
teena.tautkus@becomingme.biz
www.becomingme.biz

Teena worked within the corporate world for over 25 years. In March 2005, she left the corporate arena to embark on a new journey. In June 2005, she joined Connecticut Women Ob/Gyn as Practice Manager, where she has the opportunity to work with fabulous women every day to unfold the layers of their lives. She is an inspiring coach whose down-to-earth approach is based on her own life transformations. Her philosophy is that *anything is possible*— when you set an intention.

Teena has appeared on CBS-TV and on radio, where she had her own segment, *Tuesday's Tips from Teena.* She appeared on *Better Connecticut,* Rocky Hill, CT with Scot Haney; *Fox 61,* Hartford, CT with Rachel Lutzker, and NBC-TV's *Morning Show,* West Hartford, CT with Yvonne Nava. She is co-author of articles for *The Hartford Women's Journal* and does a monthly radio segment on the *Mary Jones Show* on WDRC 1360 AM, Hartford, CT on the second Saturday of each month, on a show entitled *Making Your Dreams Come True.*

As a Certified Dream Coach,® she speaks from the heart and believes balancing life with some fun is *fun*damental.

More Incredible Life

Now that you have learned many things about how to discover your incredible life, the next step is to take action. Get started applying what you have learned in the pages of this book.

We want you to know that we are here to help and inspire you to become your best.

Below is a list of where we are geographically located. Regardless of where our companies are located, many of us provide a variety of services over the phone or through webinars, and we welcome the opportunity to travel to your location to provide you one-on-one consulting.

You can find out more about each of us by reading our bios at the end of our chapters, or by visiting our websites, listed below.

If you are looking for one-on-one coaching or group training, many of the co-authors in this book are available to support you. Feel free to call us and let us know you have read our book and let us know how to best serve you.

California

Kimi Avary, MA	www.bulletproofwoman.com
Erin Sarika Delaney, MA, CDC	www.dreamsinmotioncoach.com
Marilyn Ellis, CTACC	www.lighthouseorganizers.com
Cori Ann Lentz, NASM CPT, ACE CPT, AFAA CPT	www.sanramonvalleyfitness.com
Jennifer Mayfield, MPA	www.jennifermayfield.com
Tammy Tribble	www.half-assedsite.com
Daria Vallentiny	www.resultscoachingalliance.com

Connecticut

Catherine Ewing-Rinker, LCSW, MDiv, RMT, CDC	www.reawakenyourdreamer.com www.spiritmattersct.com
Mary Jones	www.maryjonesshow.com
Karen Roche, CDC	www.theinnerkur.com
Teena Tautkus, CDC	www.becomingme.biz

Florida

Regena Schwarz Garrepy, CDC, CDCGL, RCS, NLC	www.reclaimyouressence.com www.livingbydesignusa.org

Massachusetts

Maura Cronin, CDC, LMP   www.mauracronin.com

Minnesota

Jan McDonough, CDC, CDCGL,   www.attitudeadventures.com
CEL, WABC

Oregon

Sheryl Eldene, MA, MBA, PCC   www.oplcenter.com

Washington

Kim Crumpler   www.uniquelysavvy.com

Michele Rastovich, CDC   www.bringyourbestself.com

Carol Stanley   www.carolstanley.com

Dr. Michelle Turcotte, ND   www.avikai.com

Debbie Whitlock   www.debbiewhitlock.com
                                www.soundfinancialpartners.com

PowerDynamics Publishing develops books for experts who want to share their knowledge with more and more people. We provide our co-authors with a proven system, professional guidance and support, producing quality, multi-author, how-to books that uplift and enhance the personal and professional lives of the people they serve.

We know that getting a book written and published is a huge undertaking. To make that process as easy as possible, we have an experienced team with the resources and know-how to put a quality, informative book in the hands of our co-authors quickly and affordably. Our co-authors are proud to be included in PowerDynamics Publishing books because these publications enhance their business missions, give them a professional outreach tool and enable them to communicate essential information to a wider audience.

You can find out more about our upcoming book projects at
www.powerdynamicspub.com

Also from
PowerDynamics Publishing

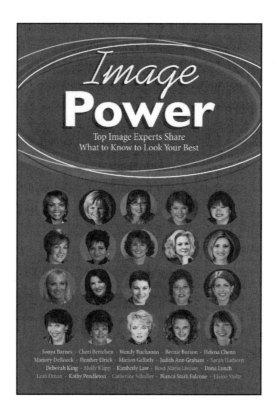

For more information on this book visit:
www.imagepowerbook.com

Also from
PowerDynamics Publishing

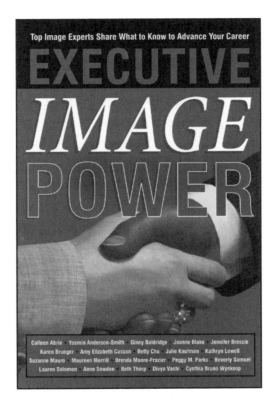

For more information on this book visit:
www.executiveimagebook.com

Also from
PowerDynamics Publishing

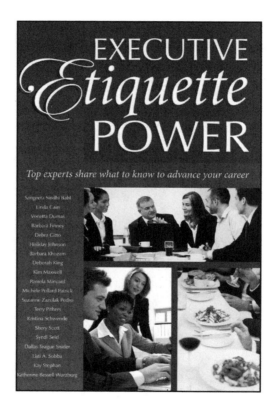

For more information on this book visit:
www.execetiquette.com

Also from
PowerDynamics Publishing

For more information on this book visit:
www.directsellingbook.com or **www.dswa.org**

Also from
PowerDynamics Publishing

TOP IMAGE EXPERTS
reveal strategies to always
look and be your best

INSPIRED
Style

Ginny Baldridge · Michele Bayle · Shirley Borrelli · Mari Bowlin
Chris Fulkerson · Pat Gray · Milena Joy · Barbara Layne · Carrie Leum
Julie Maeder · Lisa Ann Martin · Teresa McCarthy · Cynthia Lee Miller
Oreet Mizrahi · Sandy Moore · Cheryl Obermiller · Deborah Reynolds
Sally Templeton · Dominique Vaughan-Russell · Alison Vaughn · Debbie Wright

For more information on this book visit:
www.inspiredstylebook.com

Also from
PowerDynamics Publishing

Get Organized TODAY
Top experts share strategies that work

Toni Ahlgren · Anne Blumer
Nancy Castelli · Gretchen Ditto · Rhonda Elliott
Bibi Goldstein · Katie Munoz · Mary L. Noble
Tina Oscar · Natasha Packer · Scott Roewer
Janet Schiesl · JoAnn Scordino · Anna Sicalides
Melissa Stacey · Charlotte Steill · Sandy Stelter
Angela F. Wallace · Annette Watz

For more information on this book visit:
www.getorganizedtodaybook.com

For more information on any of these books visit:
www.powerdynamicspub.com

Incredible *Life*

Top experts reveal how to create yours

Kimi Avary • Maura Cronin • Kim Crumpler • Erin Sarika Delaney
Sheryl Eldene • Marilyn Ellis • Catherine Ewing-Rinker • Mary Jones
Cori Ann Lentz • Jan McDonough • Jennifer Mayfield • Michele Rastovich
Karen Roche • Regena Schwarz Garrepy • Carol Stanley • Teena Tautkus
Tammy Tribble • Michelle Turcotte • Dana Vallentiny • Debbie Whitlock

For more copies of *Incredible Life*,
contact any of the co-authors or visit
www.incrediblelifebook.com